A TASTE OF THE

MEDITERRANEAN

(MEATLESS RECIPES)

BY

ALBERT AND CHARLENE MALOOF

Over 75 recipes have **zero cholesterol** and low fat

Each recipe has nutrition facts.

Reference Sources:
Family and Friends
Wikipedia
Nutri – facts

INTRODUCTION

After we successfully published our first cookbook (A Guide to Healthy Middle Eastern Meatless Food) and based on requests from our readers, we felt obligated to publish for them and for food lovers this revised cookbook (A Taste of the Mediterranean). In order to clarify the title, most of the recipes in this book are Syrian, Lebanese, Palestinian and other countries that are on the Mediterranean and in the Middle East.

When you go through the book and cook a recipe, you will find that not only taste matters but also the health benefits of consuming this kind of food.

Also, you will find that most of the meals are a balanced diet and contain the nutrition you need: the protein in the beans, the carbohydrate in the rice and the fiber in the vegetables are gathered in one dish.

I remember that when I was a child my mom insisted to include thyme mixture (zaatar) and olive oil in my diet especially during school days and she always claimed that the thyme mixture (zaatar) is good for the brain.

As a child, what did I know? In my research, I found out that thyme leaves contain chemicals that strengthen the body and the brain's memory.

Very clearly, you will see under every recipe the nutrition facts. This way you know what you are consuming. When I was a young adult, I traveled from Syria to Iraq, then Lebanon, and also to Kuwait seeking work and for economic reasons, I was encouraged to cook at home under the direction of my mother, Julia.

But, when I came to the United States and married my wife Charlene, I found her interested in cooking Mediterranean also -- recipes that she obtained from her mother, Claire, and her grandmother Chafica.

With this knowledge and experience, we were able to publish this complete meatless cookbook. We hope it will meet your expectations.

Albert and Charlene Maloof

CONTENTS

PASTRIES AND SWEETS 63

PASTRY DOUGH STUFFED WITH WALNUTS (maamool bil joz) 76
SESAME SEED COOKIES (barazek) 77
SPICED BISCUITS (kaak bharat) 78
STUFFED FILLO DOUGH WITH RICOTTA (m'tabbak) 79
STUFFED PANCAKE (atayef) 80
SUGAR COOKIES (ghraybeh) 81
SUGAR SYRUP (attir) 82
TURMERIC COFFEE CAKE (s'foof) 83
LEFT BLANK (intentionally) 84

PICKLING 85

CRUSHED GREEN OLIVES (zaitoun m'faash) 86
PICKLING CUCUMBER (kh'yar) 87
PICKLING EGGPLANTS (baitinjan) 88
TURNIPS (liffit) 89
SLIT BLACK OR KALAMATA OLIVES (zaitoon m'jarrah) 90
STUFFED EGGPLANT (makdoos) 91
STUFFED BELL PEPPERS (flaifleh mihshieh) 92

PUDDINGS AND ICE CREAM 93

CREAM - HOMEMADE (ishta) 94
PUDDING TRAY (aish el saraya) 95
RICE PUDDING (riz bil haleeb) 96
SYRIAN ICE CREAM (booza) 97
LEFT BLANK (intentionally) 98

SALADS AND SPREADS 99

ARABIC GARDEN SALAD (salata Arabee) 100
BBQ EGGPLANT SALAD (baba ghannouj) 101
BBQ EGGPLANT SPREAD (m'tabbal) 102
BEET SALAD (salatet shawander) 103
CABBAGE SALAD (salatet yakhana) 104
CUCUMBER AND YOGURT SALAD (khiar oo laban) 105
FAVA BEANS SALAD (fool m'dammas) 106

SOUPS 115

BREADS AND PIES

PITA BREAD (khubiz)

INGREDIENTS:
2 lbs. all-purpose flour, 1 tbsp. or one envelope dry yeast
2 cups lukewarm water, 1 tsp. salt, ¼ tsp. sugar

MAKING THE DOUGH AND BAKING:
Dissolve the yeast in ¼ cup lukewarm water, and sprinkle with sugar, cover and let it rise.
Mix flour and salt in a dough mixing machine or in a large bowl. Add the yeast, the water and start mixing and kneading until the dough is firm and smooth. (During the kneading, add more water if required). Cover the dough with a cloth and set aside to rise for one to two hours or until almost double the size. Cut the dough to four ounce pieces; roll each piece between your palms to make small balls, lay the balls on a flour dusted lining cover and set aside for half an hour to rise again. On a flat surface dusted with flour, flatten each ball with a dough pin to about 6 to 7 inches in diameter and place it on a flour dusted baking tray. Cover with a cloth and set aside for two hours to rise. If you want sesame pita bread, after you flatten the dough, brush with water, and sprinkle with the sesame seeds and pat lightly. Preheat the oven to 500 degrees and bake for seven to ten minutes or until the loaf puffs up and is a light golden brown in color. Take it out from the oven and let it cool before you store it in plastic bags.

SERVING SIZE: 1.25 oz. (1/2 a loaf)
TOTAL SERVINGS: eight

AMOUNT PER SERVING:

Calories	98.00 kcal
Total fat	1.00 g
Cholesterol	0.00 mg
Sodium	150.00 mg
Total carbohydrate	20.00 g
Dietary fiber	1.00 g
Protein	2.00 g

NOTE:
You can freeze the bread for a long time. Pita bread, Arabic bread, Syrian bread, pocket bread -- whatever we call it -- is healthy and is practical and you can eat it just like that or next to a meal or stuff it with falafel, kabobs, hummus or with most Middle Eastern foods.

BASIC DOUGH FOR PIES 1 (ajeenet fatayer)

INGREDIENTS:
1 lb. flour
1 cup lukewarm water
½ tsp. salt
1envelope dry yeast
¼ tsp. sugar
¼ tsp. mahlab (black cherry kernels) (optional)

PREPARATION:
Dissolve yeast in ¼ cup warm water, sprinkle with sugar, cover and set it aside to rise.
Place the flour in a large mixing bowl or in a dough mixing machine adding salt, yeast, water and mahlab if desired and mix well.
Knead until the dough is firm and smooth in texture.
Dust the top of the dough with flour or rub the top of the dough with olive oil.
Cover with plastic wrap and a towel and let rise for two hours or until it is almost double in size.
Now the dough is ready to divide the way you want according to the recipe.

SERVING SIZE: one ounce
TOTAL SERVINGS: 28 ounces

AMOUNT PER SERVING:

Calories	15.69 kcal
Total fat	0.00 g
Cholesterol	0.00 mg
Sodium	83.59 mg
Total carbohydrate	3.36 g
Dietary Fiber	0.21 g
Protein	0.44 g

NOTE:
You can use this dough for all kinds of pies unless otherwise specified in the recipe.
You can freeze the dough, and then when you defrost it let it stand at room temperature to rise.
Also you can divide the dough to two-ounce pieces to make a larger pie.

BASIC DOUGH FOR PIES 2 (ajeenet fatayer)

INGREDIENTS:

1 lb. flour
½ cup low fat milk
¼ cup water
¼ cup olive oil
½ tsp. salt
1 envelope dry yeast
¼ cup lukewarm water
¼ tsp. sugar

PREPARATION:

Dissolve the yeast in ¼ cup lukewarm water, sprinkle with sugar, cover and set it aside to rise.
Place the flour in a large bowl or in a dough mixing machine adding salt, yeast, water, milk, ¼ cup water and olive oil and mix well.
Knead until the dough is firm and smooth in texture. Rub the top of the dough with olive oil.
Cover with plastic wrap and a towel and let rise for two hours or until almost double in size.
Now the dough is ready to divide the way you want according to the recipe.

SERVING SIZE: one ounce
TOTAL SERVINGS: 28 ounces

AMOUNT PER SERVING:

Calories	35.23 kcal
Total fat	2.00 g
Cholesterol	0.35 mg
Sodium	23.72 mg
Total carbohydrate	3.61 g
Dietary Fiber	0.23 g
Protein	0.44 g

NOTE:

You can use this dough for all kinds of pies unless otherwise specified in the recipe. You can freeze the dough, and then when you defrost it let it stand at room temperature to rise. Also you can divide the dough to 12 pieces to make a larger pie.

CHEESE PIES (fatayer bil jebin)

INGREDIENTS:

Basic dough for pies 1 (28 ounces)
½ lb. Syrian white cheese (chopped fine)
½ lb. feta cheese (chopped fine)
½ cup chopped parsley
½ cup chopped onion
½ tsp. salt, ½ tsp. allspice

STUFFING AND BAKING:

Mix all the ingredients together except the dough and divide them into 14 parts. On a flour-dusted surface divide the dough to fourteen parts, and then flatten each dough part into an oval shape and place on a greased baking tray. Place one part of the stuffing on the center of the flattened dough. Pinch the two opposite ends of the dough to make a boat shape pie (see picture). Bake the pies in a preheated oven at 350 degrees for 15 minutes on the lower shelf and ten minutes on the upper shelf , or until the edges are golden brown. Serve at room temperature.

SERVING SIZE: one
TOTAL SERVINGS: fourteen

AMOUNT PER SERVING:

Calories	131.70 kcal
Total fat	8.66 g
Cholesterol	31.42 mg
Sodium	538.32 mg
Total carbohydrate	8.50 g
Dietary fiber	0.58 g
Protein	196.48 g

NOTE:

You can change the shape of the pie: you can make it the size of a cookie as an appetizer for a party. This way you can divide the dough to ninety or one hundred twenty pieces.
Or, you can make them round like small pizza pies. Syrian white cheese is available at most Middle Eastern grocery stores.

HOLY BREAD (kurban)

INGREDIENTS:
Recipe (basic dough 1-28 ounces)

PREPARING & BAKING:
Making this recipe of basic dough is enough for one loaf of Holy Bread only.
If the parish is large, double or triple the recipe.
Place the dough on flour dusted baking tray and press it down with your palm to flatten it a bit.
Stamp the dough firmly with the Holy bread stamp.
With a toothpick, pinch the dough in several places to prevent from rising in the oven during baking.
Bake in a preheated oven at 400 degrees for 20 to 30 minutes or until the bottom of the loaf is a light golden brown in color.
Remove from the oven and brush the surface with cold water and then let it dry.

SERVING SIZE: one ounce
TOTAL SERVINGS: twenty four

AMOUNT PER SERVING:

Calorie	15.68 kcal
Total fat	0.00 g
Cholesterol	0.00 mg
Sodium	23.57 mg
Total carbohydrate	3.36 g
Dietary fiber	0.21 g
Protein	0.43 g

Holy Bread stamp

NOTE:
The Holy Bread, "Prosforo", the literal translation is "offering" and that is precisely what it is: an offering of your faith to GOD. Before the liturgy service starts, the priest breaks some of the Holy Bread with a special prayer and places them in the holy chalice for the Communion. The Eastern Rite Orthodox faithful believe through the invocation of the Holy Spirit the bread and wine will be transformed into the body and blood of CHRIST.

SPINACH PIES (fatayer sabanegh)

INGREDIENTS:

Double basic dough for Pies 1 divided into twenty-eight pieces
2 ½ lbs. fresh spinach, washed, chopped and spread on towel paper to dry overnight
2 cups diced onion, ½ cup chopped walnuts
2 tsp. salt and 1 tsp. allspice (bharat), 1 tbsp. sumac
¾ cup olive oil, ¾ cup lemon juice

BAKING:

Roll each part of dough between your palms to form dough balls and place on a flour dusted tray.
Dust the top of the dough balls with flour and cover with plastic wrap and a towel; set aside in a warm place for about 30 minutes to rise. Mix all the ingredients together (without the dough) divide into 28 parts. Flatten each dough ball with a dough pin to 4-5 inches in diameter. Place the flattened dough on a plate and place one part of the spinach mixture in the center of the flattened dough. Fold three sides of the dough over to make it a triangle shape and press the edges together to seal. Place on a greased baking tray; bake in a preheated oven at 400 degrees for 20 minutes on the lower rack and 15 minutes on the upper rack or until the surface of the pies are golden brown. Let cool to a room temperature and serve.

SERVING SIZE: one pie
TOTAL SERVINGS: twenty eight

AMOUNT PER SERVING:

Calories	97.13 kcal
Total fat	7.35 g
Cholesterol	0.00 mg
Sodium	198.72 mg
Total carbohydrate	6.68 g
Dietary Fiber	1.72 g
Protein	2.51 g

NOTE:

Serve at room temperature. Spinach has a high nutritional value and is extremely rich in antioxidants. It is a rich source of Vitamin A, Vitamin C, Vitamin E, Vitamin K, magnesium, manganese, folate, iron, calcium, potassium, Vitamin B_2, Vitamin B_6, folic acid, copper, protein, phosphorus, zinc, niacin, selenium, also Omega 3 fatty acids. You can freeze the pies for future use.

THYME PIE (mana'eesh zaatar)

INGREDIENTS:

18 oz. pie dough (dough for Pies 1)
1/2 cup olive oil
3/4 cup zaatar (see Note)

BAKING:

Mix oil and zaatar together and set aside. Sprinkle 16" diameter baking tray with flour. On a flat flour dusted surface, roll the dough to 16" inches in diameter and place it in the tray. Pour the zaatar mixture in the center of the tray and spread it all over the dough. Press down the mixture in the dough all over with your fingers. (The other option is to cut the dough to eight pieces and flatten each piece individually; spread the mixture on the top and bake) or cut the dough to 16 pieces to make them cocktail size. Preheat the oven to 400 degrees.
Bake the pie for 15 minutes. Take it out and cut it with a pizza cutter to eight pieces.
Serve it hot.

SERVING SIZE: one
TOTAL SERVINGS: eight

AMOUNT PER SERVING:

Calories	159.00 kcal
Total fat	16.00 g
Cholesterol	0.00 mg
Sodium	43.00 mg
Total carbohydrate	0.80 g
Dietary Fiber	3.00 g
Protein	1.00 g

NOTE:

Zaatar is a spice plant with small green leaves (thyme). The dried crushed thyme leaves with other spices, bread crumbs and other seeds makes the zaatar that we used for this recipe (mana'eesh). Zaatar has a health value; as a matter a fact, in Syria and Lebanon, Palestine and other Middle Eastern countries the parents encourage their children to have a "zait oo zaatar sandwich" in the morning before they go to school and before taking an exam. They believe that the zaatar is good for the brain memory and for the strength of the body (see making zaatar). Also, you can get ready made pizza dough and use it for mana'eesh. Zaatar is sold at Middle Eastern grocery stores.

CANDIES, JAMS AND PRESERVES

APRICOT JAM (marmalad)

INGREDIENTS:
2 lbs. fresh ripened apricots, 2 lbs. sugar

COOKING:
Wash the apricots and set aside to dry. Split open the apricots; remove and discard the pits.
With your hand, crush and mash the apricots. Place a strainer over a pot and place cheesecloth over the strainer and pour the mashed apricots in. Wrap the cheesecloth to make it like a sack. Hold the sack from the neck with one hand and squeeze the juice out of the sack with the other hand; discard the stringy pieces left over from the apricots inside the sack after you finish squeezing the juice out. Remove the strainer and cheesecloth from the pot. Add the sugar to the apricot juice that was squeezed into the pot and mix well. On high heat, bring the apricot juice to a boil. Then reduce the heat to low and simmer for fifteen minutes. During the process of cooking, skim the froth from the top of the mixture and discard. Pour the apricot mixture into a two inch high tray edge and place a bottle filled with water and capped in the middle of the tray. Cover the tray with thin cheesecloth; place the tray on a table in a sunny area. (See picture.) Place the legs of the table in containers full of water to prevent ants from getting to the tray. Bring the tray indoors every evening to mix the apricots; then take out into the sun the next morning. Repeat the process for three days or until the jam thickens. Place the jam in clean glass jars. Preferably, keep refrigerated.

SERVING SIZE: one tablespoon
TOTAL SERVINGS: see below

AMOUNT PER SERVING:

Calories	60.00 kcal
Total fat	0.00 g
Cholesterol	0.00 mg
Sodium	0.00 mg
Total carbohydrate	14.00 g
Dietary fiber	0.00 g
Protein	0.00 g

NOTE:
The apricots contain Vitamin A, Vitamin C, beta carotene, and Iron. The top eleven countries of apricot quantity production are Turkey, Iran, Italy, Pakistan, Greece, France, Algeria, Spain, Japan, Morocco, and Syria.
Total servings: depends on the amount of apricots you make.

APRICOT PRESERVES (m'rabba al mishmosh)

INGREDIENTS:
4 LBS. APRICOTS
3 1/2 lbs. sugar

PREPARATION:
Wash the apricots and set them aside to dry, then split them in half and remove the pits and discard. Place the apricots in a tray, add the sugar and mix well.
Spread them out in the tray and place a bottle filled with water and capped in the middle of the tray. Cover the tray with thin cheesecloth (see apricot jam picture) and place the tray on a table in a very sunny area. Place the legs of the table in containers full of water to prevent ants from getting to the tray.
Bring the tray indoors every evening to mix the apricots; then take out into the sun the next morning. Repeat the process for three days or until the preserves gets thickened.
Place the preserves in clean glass jars.
Preferably keep refrigerated.

SERVING SIZE: one tablespoon
TOTAL SERVINGS: see below

AMOUNT PER SERVING:	
Calories	60.00 kcal
Total fat	0.00 g
Cholesterol	0.00 mg
Sodium	0.00 mg
Total carbohydrate	14.00 g
Dietary fiber	0.00 g
Protein	0.00 g

NOTE:
The apricots contain Vitamin A, Vitamin C, beta carotene, and Iron.
The top eleven countries of apricot quantity production are Turkey, Iran, Italy, Pakistan, Greece, France, Algeria, Spain, Japan, Morocco, and Syria.
Total servings: based on the amount you make: one, two, three or four pounds.

EGGPLANT PRESERVES (m'rabba el'baitinjan)

INGREDIENTS:

2 lbs. small peeled eggplants (Japanese about 60 eggplants)
¼ cup pickling lime powder and ½ a gallon water, 1/4 cup lemon juice
6 cups sugar; 3 cups water; 60 cloves; tangerine peel or orange peel

COOKING:

Dissolve pickling lime with a ½ gallon of water in a glass container and set aside for the lime to settle at the bottom of the container. Place the eggplants in another glass container and pour the clear lime water from the other container over them and set aside for overnight. Discard the lime that settled in the bottom of the first container. Drain the lime water from the eggplants and rinse them several times. Place the eggplants in a cooking pot; cover with water and bring to a boil. Cook for five minutes. Drain the eggplants and set aside to cool to the point that you can hold one in your hand, slit the side of the eggplants and gently squeeze each one to get the liquid out and then insert one clove in each one. In a cooking pot, place six cups sugar, three cups water, a few pieces of tangerine peel and the lemon juice. Bring to a boil and cook on medium heat for five minutes or until it becomes syrupy. Add the eggplants to the sugar syrup and let them cook on low to medium heat for forty-five minutes or until the syrup thickens. Remove from the stove and set aside to cool. Store the eggplants with the syrup in a clean glass jar; discard the tangerine or orange peel.

SERVING SIZE: one
TOTAL SERVINGS: sixty

AMOUNT PER SERVING:

Calories	81.91 kcal
Total fat	0.03 g
Cholesterol	0.00 mg
Sodium	0.61 mg
Total carbohydrate	21.08 g
Dietary fiber	0.38 g
Protein	0.13 g

NOTE:

The eggplant originated in India. The Arabic name is "baitinjan". Eggplant was introduced throughout the Mediterranean area by the Arabs in the early middle Ages. Studies of the Institute of Sao Paulo State University, Brazil, have shown that eggplant is effective in the treatment of high blood cholesterol but cannot replace statin drugs. In the Arab world, eggplant is used in many different dishes.

FIG JAM (m'rabba al teen)

INGREDIENTS:
1 lb. dried figs
1/2 lb. sugar
½ cup crushed walnuts
1 tsp. ground anise seeds
1 tbsp. sesame seeds
1 tbsp. lemon juice
½ tsp. Arabic gum (finely ground)
1 cup water

MAKING:
Wash the figs with cold water then remove the stems from the figs and discard. Cut each fig to four pieces and place in a four quart pot and add one cup of water and the sugar and soak them overnight.
On high heat, bring the mixture to a boil then reduce the heat to low and cook for half an hour. Add to the pot the walnuts, sesame seeds, anise seeds and the Arabic gum.
Mix the combination and let it simmer for another ten minutes.
Remove from the stove, mix in the lemon juice and set aside to cool.
Place in a clean glass jar.

SERVING SIZE: one ounce
TOTAL SERVINGS: thirty six

AMOUNT PER SERVING:
Calories	209.53 kcal
Total fat	1.00 g
Cholesterol	0.00 mg
Sodium	1.68 mg
Total carbohydrate	14.90 g
Dietary fiber	1.66 g
Protein	0.63 g

NOTE:
Figs are one of the highest plant sources of Calcium and Fiber. According to the USDA data for mission variety figs, green figs are richest in fiber, copper, manganese, magnesium, calcium and Vitamin K. Figs have a laxative effect and contain antioxidants.

ORANGE MARMALADE (m'rabba al bourtukhal)

INGREDIENTS:
4 large oranges, about three pounds
Finely grated zest of two lemons
Juice of two lemons
5 cups sugar
4 cups water

COOKING:
Wash the oranges and lemons very well.
Place 4 cups of water in a large stainless steel pot.
Cut off the top and bottom of the oranges and discard.
Slice the oranges into one inch slices discarding pits. Cut every slice into four quarters.
Grate the lemons to a fine zest. Place 4 cups of water, the lemon zest and the oranges into a pot. Bring the mixture to a boil and keep it boiling for fifteen minutes. Reduce the heat to medium. Add the sugar and the lemon juice to the mixture and let it cook for ninety minutes or until the mixture is thickened.
Stir the mixture from time to time during the cooking process.
Store in clean glass jars; cover tightly. Let cool, then refrigerate or keep in a cool place.

SERVING SIZE: one ounce
TOTAL SERVINGS: ninety eight

_____

AMOUNT PER SERVING:
Calories	48.10 kcal
Total fat	0.10 g
Cholesterol	0.00 mg
Sodium	0.26 mg
Total carbohydrate	12.13 g
Dietary fiber	35.37 g
Protein	1.54 g

NOTE:
Serve with cream cheese on toast or with butter on toast.
Oranges are a source of Vitamin C, potassium, thiamine, phosphorus, folic aside, Vitamin B_9, and Vitamin B_6.

PONDEROSA LEMON RIND PRESERVES (kibbad)

INGREDIENTS:
¼ cup pickling lime and ½ gallon water
2 large ponderosa lemons (about 2 ½ lbs.)
2 ½ lbs. sugar
3 cups water
¼ cup lemon juice
1/8 cup orange blossom water

COOKING:
Rinse the ponderosa lemons and grate the outside skin and discard the zest. Cut each lemon into four parts. Remove the inside of the lemons and squeeze them to be used in the future as lemon juice. Cut the rinds into 85 pieces. Dissolve 1/4 cup pickling lime powder with ½ gallon water in a glass container; stir a few times and let it settle. Remove the clear lime water to another pot and discard the lime that settled in the bottom of the container. Place the rind pieces in the lime water and set aside for overnight or at least eight hours. Drain and rinse the rind several times with fresh water. Place the rind pieces in a large pot, cover with water and bring to a boil. Then, reduce the heat to medium and cook for 35 minutes. Remove the pieces from the water and set aside to cool. With your hand squeeze the water out of each one of the rinds and set aside again. In another large pot, place three cups of water, the sugar and lemon juice and bring to a boil to make syrup. Add the rind pieces to the syrup and bring to a boil again; reduce the heat to medium and cook until the syrup thickens. Add the orange blossom water and remove the pot from the stove and set aside to cool. Place the rinds with the syrup in a clean glass jar.

SERVING SIZE: one piece
TOTAL SERVINGS: eighty five

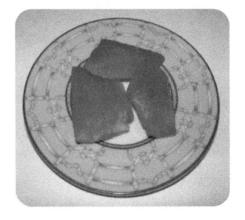

AMOUNT PER SERVING:
Calories	20.85 kcal
Total fat	0.00 g
Cholesterol	0.00 mg
Sodium	0.05 mg
Total carbohydrate	5.42 g
Dietary fiber	0.00 g
Protein	0.00 g

NOTE
You could refrigerate the kibbad or leave it out in a cool place.

PUMPKIN PRESERVES CUBES (m'rabba al yaateen)

INGREDIENTS:

2 lbs. fresh pumpkin
¼ cup pickling lime and ½ gallon cold water
4 cups sugar
1/4 cup lemon juice, 2 cups hot water
25 cloves

COOKING:

Cut the pumpkin in half and remove the seeds and the stringy layers from inside.
Peel the skin off and cut the pumpkin into forty six cubes and set aside.
In a glass container, place ½ gallon of water and the lime, mix very well, then, pour the lime water mixture over the pumpkin and set aside overnight. The next day, drain the lime water and replace it with fresh water. Soak the pumpkin for one day changing the water several times until you see the water is not cloudy anymore. Then, drain the water and spread the pumpkin on clean material for two hours to dry. Place the pumpkin in a large pot; add the sugar and mix and set aside overnight for the sugar to extract the liquid from the pumpkin. The next day add two cups of water, the cloves and the lemon juice to the pot and bring to a boil.
Reduce the heat to low to medium and cook for seventy five minutes or until the syrup thickens. Remove from the stove and set aside to cool; then place the pumpkin with the syrup in a clean glass jar.

SERVING SIZE: one ounce
TOTAL SERVINGS: forty six

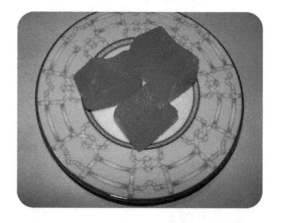

_____
AMOUNT PER SERVING:

Calories	64.16 kcal
Total fat	0.10 g
Cholesterol	0.00 mg
Sodium	0.32 mg
Total carbohydrate	16.51 g
Dietary fiber	0.17 g
Protein	0.11 g

NOTE:

Pumpkin is high in Vitamin A and beta carotene. Also pumpkin contains Vitamin B, thiamine, riboflavin, niacin, folate, Vitamin C, Vitamin E, calcium, iron, magnesium, phosphorus and potassium.

QUINCE JAM (m'rabba el'safargel)

INGREDIENTS:
2 lbs. fresh quince grated
2 lbs. sugar
1 tbsp. lemon juice (optional)

MAKING:
On a large tray, spread the grated quince and set aside for an hour until the color becomes reddish pink. Add the sugar, mix well and set aside for another hour.
Place the mixture into a three quart pot and cook on low to medium heat until the mixture thickens and turns a golden red color.
Stir the mixture from time to time during the cooking process.
Mix in the lemon juice and let it cool.
Transfer the jam to your choice of glass jar or container; refrigeration optional.
Enjoy with cream cheese on toasted bread.

SERVING SIZE: one ounce
TOTAL SERVING: forty six

_____

AMOUNT PER SERVING:

Calories	109.96 kcal
Total fat	0.02 g
Cholesterol	0.00 mg
Sodium	0.99 mg
Total carbohydrate	22.89 g
Dietary fiber	0.38 g
Protein	0.08 g

NOTE:
Quince contains folate, Vitamin C, calcium, iron, magnesium, phosphorus and potassium.
You can enjoy eating fresh quince when it thoroughly ripens.
Quince jam is delicious on toasted bread with cream cheese.

QUINCE PRESERVES (Safargel sha'af)

INGREDIENTS:
2 lbs. fresh quince
2 lbs. sugar
1 tbsp. lemon juice (optional)

MAKING:
Wash the quince and cut each one to eight pieces.
Peel the skin and remove the core from inside each piece.
Mix the quince and the sugar together and set aside overnight or for at least four hours for the sugar to extract the liquid from the quince.
Add the mixture to a cooking pot and bring to a boil.
Cook on low to medium heat until the syrup thickens and the quince turns dark pink to red in color (see the picture below).
Add the lemon juice and let it cool.
Transfer the quince to your choice of glass jar or container.
Enjoy as a dessert.

SERVING SIZE: one ounce
TOTAL SERVING: forty six

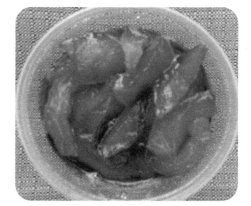

AMOUNT PER SERVING:

Calories	109.96 kcal
Total fat	0.02 g
Cholesterol	0.00 mg
Sodium	0.99 mg
Total carbohydrate	22.89 g
Dietary fiber	0.38 g
Protein	0.08 g

NOTE:
Quince can be eaten raw when it is thoroughly ripened.
Also, it can be roasted, baked or stewed.
Quince is high in Vitamin A and potassium.
You follow the same method to make apple preserves.

STRAWBERRY JAM (m'rabba al' fraiz)

INGREDIENTS:
1 lb. strawberries (yield 3 cups)
¾ lb. sugar
¼ cup lemon juice
3 tbsp. brandy
Zest of one orange, finely grated
¼ cup crushed walnuts

COOKING:
Rinse the strawberries and remove the green stems and discard.
Cut each strawberry into four quarters.
Place the strawberries in a stainless steel pot. Add the sugar, the orange zest and set aside for 30 minutes.
Bring to a gentle boil for about twenty minutes; skim the froth as it appears.
Keep boiling until the jam thickens.
Test the jam by dropping a little jam on a chilled plate, tilt the plate and if the jam runs it means the jam is not ready.
When the jam is ready, add to it the brandy, lemon juice, walnuts and mix.
Place in clean glass jars and cover tightly.
Keep the jam in a cool place or in the refrigerator.

SERVING SIZE: one ounce
TOTAL SERVINGS: sixteen

AMOUNT PER SERVING:

Calories	77.00 kcal
Total fat	0.00 g
Cholesterol	0.00 mg
Sodium	1.00 mg
Total carbohydrate	20.00 g
Dietary fiber	0.00 g
Protein	0.00 g

NOTE:
Strawberries contain iron, magnesium, phosphorus, calcium, potassium, zinc, copper, thiamin, riboflavin, niacin, and Vitamins C, B_6, B_{12}, A, and E.

TURKISH DELIGHT (raha halloum)

INGREDIENTS:
3 tbsp. gelatin, 1 1/2 cups corn starch
¼ cup rose water, 3 cups sugar
¼ cup powdered sugar
½ cup skinned and crushed pistachio nuts

MAKING:
Take an 8"x 8" greased tray and cover the inside with plastic wrap, then grease the plastic wrap with light oil or cooking spray. In ¼ cup cold water, stir the corn starch very well and set aside. In ½ cup cold water sprinkle the gelatin to soften and set aside. Place 1½ cups of water in a cooking pot, stir in the sugar and rose water and bring to a boil stirring until the sugar is dissolved. Reduce the heat to medium, and then add gelatin and corn starch and stir about ten minutes or until the mixture gets very thick. Stir in the pistachios for one minute; then pour it in the tray smoothing the top and cover loosely. Chill for about four hours. On a smooth work surface, sift one tablespoon of powdered sugar to cover the size of the tray. Remove the cover from the tray and turn it over the powdered working surface. Remove the rest of the wrap and discard it. Cut the raha into one inch squares. Store the raha in a container and sprinkle with the rest of the powdered sugar gently tossing to coat all cubes. Wrap the raha with plastic wrap and chill.

SERVING SIZE: one
TOTAL SERVINGS: sixty four

AMOUNT PER SERVING:	
Calories	40.00 kcal
Total fat	1.50 g
Cholesterol	0.00 mg
Sodium	0.00 mg
Total carbohydrate	16.50 g
Dietary fiber	0.00 g
Protein	0.00 g

NOTE:
Turkish delight (locum) was introduced to the Middle East at the time of the Ottoman Empire since the 15th century. The Turkish word (locum) comes from the Arabic (luqma) mouthful.
Raha halloum in Arabic means contentment of the throat.

MEATLESS

BAKED SPAGHETTI (macaroneh bil'firin)

INGREDIENTS:
1 lb. thin spaghetti (boiled with 1 tbsp. oil, then drained)
1 large onion (chopped)
1 cans tomato sauce (15 oz.)
1 can Mexican or Italian style stewed tomatoes (14.5 oz.), chopped fine
½ cup olive oil
1 tsp. salt
1 tsp. allspice
1 cup water

BAKING:
Sauté the onion with the oil until the onion becomes translucent and soft.
Add water, tomato sauce, stewed tomatoes, salt, allspice and simmer on medium heat for thirty minutes.
Place the cooked and drained spaghetti in a baking tray and add the tomato mixture and mix well, add some water if you think it needs it.
Place the tray under the broiler for about ten minutes (optional – garnish with parmesan cheese before placing in the oven).

SERVING SIZE: one cup
TOTAL SERVINGS: thirteen

AMOUNT PER SERVING:

Calories	48.45 kcal
Total fat	4.44 g
Cholesterol	0.00 mg
Sodium	366.00 mg
Total carbohydrate	14.15 g
Dietary fiber	1.55 g
Protein	2.32 g

NOTE:
Serve hot next to Arabic green salad and pita bread.

BULGUR WITH TOMATOES (burghul oo banadora)

INGREDIENTS:
2 cups bulgur #4
3 tbsp. tomato paste
2 cups water
1 can Mexican or Italian stewed tomatoes (14 ½ ounces) chop in the blender
1 can garbanzo beans, drained and rinsed
¼ cup olive oil
2 medium size onions (diced)
1 tsp. salt and 1 tsp. allspices

COOKING:
Dissolve the tomato paste in two cups of water and set aside.
Combine onions, oil, salt and allspices and sauté on medium heat until the onions become opaque and tender.
Add the bulgur to the onions and sauté for another ten minutes.
Add to the pot the garbanzo beans, chopped tomatoes, the dissolved tomato paste mixture and bring to a boil.
Reduce the heat and cover the pot. Simmer for 30 to 35 minutes or until the bulgur are cooked well and the liquid is absorbed. Place in a serving platter and serve hot or at room temperature.

SERVING SIZE: one cup
TOTAL SERVINGS: eight

AMOUNT PER SERVING:

Calories	159.94 kcal
Total fat	7.50 g
Cholesterol	0.00 mg
Sodium	467.08 mg
Total carbohydrate	23.64 g
Dietary fiber	5.47 g
Protein	5.85 g

NOTE:
You can substitute the bulgur with rice and use the same method of cooking.

BULGUR PILAF (burghul m'falfal)

INGREDIENTS:
1 cup #4 bulgur,
2 cups water
¼ cup I can't believe It's Not Butter! ®
¼ cup vermicelli, ½ tsp. salt

COOKING:
In a three quart pot, sauté the bulgur and vermicelli with the butter on medium heat until you see the vermicelli turn a light brown.
Add the water and salt and bring to a boil.
Reduce the heat to low, cover and let cook for about 25 to 30 minutes. Remove the pot and set aside for about five minutes.
Serve hot with other recommended meals.
Or enjoy solo with plain yogurt.

SERVING SIZE: half cup
TOTAL SERVINGS: six

AMOUNT PER SERVINGS:

Calories	132.00 kcal
Total fat	7.00 g
Cholesterol	0.00 mg
Sodium	258.20 mg
Total carbohydrate	61.60 g
Dietary Fiber	0.04 g
Protein	0.04 g

NOTE:
Bulgur is compared to enriched white rice.
Bulgur has more fiber and protein, is lower in glycemic index and higher in most vitamins and minerals. The name bulgur is from Turkish "bulgur" which came from Arabic "burghul".
The food is popular in Middle Eastern and Mediterranean dishes.
Bulgur can be used in pilafs, soups, bakery goods, in stuffing, Tabbouleh and kibbeh.
Bulgur is high in nutritional value which makes it a good substitute for rice.

Cabbage Rolls (yakhana malfoof)

INGREDIENTS:
1 head cabbage, 1/2 recipe meatless stuffing
1 tsp. dried mint leaves, 5 garlic cloves
1/8 cup lemon juice

COOKING:
In a large stainless steel pot, place the head of cabbage and cover with water; bring to a boil. Stick a long fork in the core of the cabbage (A) and with a sharp knife cut around the core to release the leaves in the boiling water, take the core out and discard. Cook the leaves for ten minutes. With a tong, remove the leaves from the water; place them in a colander to drain the water. There should be 25 leaves count, about 20 ounces total. On a flat plate, you lay one cabbage leaf and with your thumb press down the rib to make it flat. Take one heaping tablespoon of the meatless mixture and place it on the cabbage leaf, (see figure B). Fold the two sides of the leaf over and then fold the top end over and with your thumbs and fingers start rolling (C). In a large pot, lay some plain cabbage leaves at the bottom of the pot to cover it. Place the rolled cabbage leaves in the pot.

Place the garlic and the mint leaves on the top of the rolled leaves (D) and cover with more plain leaves. Cover the rolled cabbage with a large plate and a weight over it (E). Add water to the pot to the top of plate level. Bring to a boil then reduce the heat to low and cook for 90 minutes or until the rolls are tender. Shut off the heat; add the lemon juice and let the leaves cool for about ten minutes before removing from the pot.

SERVING SIZE: one roll
TOTAL SERVINGS: twenty five

AMOUNT PER SERVING:

Calories	11.32 kcal
Total fat	3 .69 g
Cholesterol	0.00 mg
Sodium	107.78 mg
Total carbohydrate	5.80 g
Dietary fiber	1.15 g
Protein	

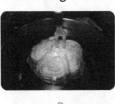
A

B

C

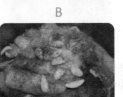
D

E

F

NOTE:
Serve hot with Arabic bread and next to radishes.

COTTAGE CHEESE (areesheh)

INGREDIENTS:

½ gallon liquid from cheese making
Or ½ gallon skimmed milk
½ gallon whole milk
¼ cup lemon juice

MAKING CHEESE:

Place the ingredients in a pot and cook on medium heat until you see the milk separate.
Place cheesecloth into a colander and place the colander over a large bowl.
Pour the milk mixture into the cheesecloth.
Remove the cottage cheese from the cheesecloth; place it on a serving plate and refrigerate.
Discard the liquid that drained into the bowl.

SERVING SIZE: one oz.
TOTAL SERVINGS: ten

AMOUNT PER SERVING:

Calories	51.00 kcal
Total fat	10.90 g
Cholesterol	4.50 mg
Sodium	229.50 mg
Total carbohydrate	2.05 g
Dietary fiber	0.00 g
Protein	31.06 g

NOTE:

You sprinkle sugar on the cheese if you like it sweet, otherwise sprinkle some salt.
The term "cottage cheese" is believed to have originated because the simple cheese was usually made in cottages from any milk leftover after making butter.
Cottage cheese is tasty, nutritious, easily digested, and low in calories.

DRIED YOGURT MEAL (kishik)

INGREDIENTS:

1 cup dried yogurt powder (kishik)
10 cups hot water, 1 cup diced onion
3 tbsp. I can't believe It's Not Butter! ®
1 cup chopped fresh cilantro and 3 cloves garlic (mashed with the salt)
1 cup chopped cabbage (boiled)
1 tsp. salt and 1 tsp. allspice, 2 tbsp. olive oil

COOKING:

Soak the dried yogurt with the water and set aside.
Sauté garlic and the cilantro with the olive oil for about five minutes and set aside.
Sauté the onion and the cabbage with the butter on medium heat until the onion is opaque and tender.
Add the soaked kishik and cook on medium heat for 30 minutes or until the mixture thickens.
The mixture should thicken slightly. Add the cilantro and garlic and cook for another 15 minutes.
Sprinkle with the allspice.
Serve hot with toasted pita bread chips.

SERVING SIZE: one cup
TOTAL SERVINGS: ten

AMOUNT PER SERVING:

Calories	87.20 kcal
Total fat	7.32 g
Cholesterol	4.10 mg
Sodium	331.88 mg
Total carbohydrate	3.57 g
Dietary fiber	0.84 g
Protein	1.20 g

NOTE:

Zahleh, a town in Lebanon, and Deir Atieh a town near Damascus, Syria, are famous for producing a delicious kishik.
Also, kishik is produced in many villages around the Middle East. Kishik is considered a winter meal. Kishik is
available at Middle Eastern grocery stores.

EGGPLANT AND GARBANZO BEAN STEW (tabback roho)

INGREDIENTS:

1 lb. eggplant, 1 can garbanzo beans (about 2 cups) rinsed
1 medium size onion, 3 cloves garlic, 1 cup tomato sauce, ¼ cup olive oil
1 tbsp. dry crumbled mint leaves, 1 tsp. salt, 2 cups of water

COOKING:

Peel the eggplant and slice it into six strips lengthwise, then cut the pieces in half.
Place the eggplant in a bowl and sprinkle with salt, set aside and let the liquid drain from the eggplant. In a stew pot, place the onions and sauté with the oil on medium to high heat for about 15 minutes until the onions become opaque and tender.
Add the eggplant and the rest of the ingredients and bring to a boil, then reduce the heat to low.
Cover and let the meal simmer for about thirty minutes or until the garbanzo beans are tender.

SERVING SIZE: half cup
TOTAL SERVINGS: eight

AMOUNT PER SERVING:

Calories	141.36 kcal
Total fat	8.04 g
Cholesterol	0.00 mg
Sodium	403.69 mg
Total carbohydrate	14.55 g
Dietary Fiber	3.43 g
Protein	4.23 g

NOTE:

Enjoy next to bulgur pilaf and radishes or plain with pita bread.
The eggplant originated in India. The Arabic name for eggplant is "baitinjan".
Eggplant was introduced throughout the Mediterranean Area by the Arabs in the early middle Ages.
Studies of the Institute of Sao Paulo State University, Brazil, have shown that eggplant is effective in the treatment of high blood cholesterol but cannot replace statin drugs.
In the Arab world, eggplant is used in many dishes as you see in different chapters of this book.

FALAFEL (falafel)

INGREDIENTS:
1 lb. dried broad fava beans, 1 lb. dried garbanzo beans
1 cup chopped onion, 5 cloves garlic, 2 tbsp. cumin, 2 tbsp. dry coriander seeds
1 tsp. salt, 1 tsp. black pepper, 1 cup chopped parsley, 1 tsp. baking powder
2 slices thick white bread, vegetable oil for frying

PREPARING AND FRYING:
Wash the fava and the garbanzo beans with cold water and soak (in water) overnight.
Next day, drain the beans and rinse thoroughly with cold water. Peel the fava beans and discard the skin. Mix the beans and the rest of the ingredients (except the parsley).
Place some of the mixture in a meat grinder and grind; repeat until you grind all of them.
Place the mixture in a large bowl, add the parsley and keep at room temperature for about two hours. Form the mixture into small balls (1/8 of a cup) then press it between your palms to make it a patty. Fry the patties in hot oil. It is easier to use the falafel tool if you have it.
You can freeze the falafel mixture in a two cup size packages.

SERVING SIZE: one falafel
TOTAL SERVINGS: forty eight

AMOUNT PER SERVING:

Calories	50.00 kcal
Total fat	3.30 g
Cholesterol	0.00 mg
Sodium	50.00 mg
Total carbohydrate	5.41 g
Dietary fiber	0.00 g
Protein	2.26 g

NOTE:
To make a falafel sandwich, cut pita bread in half, then stuff one half with three falafel patties, diced tomatoes, diced pickles, diced cucumber, and top it off with some tarator (tahineh sauce - see recipe). Because of the garbanzo bean ingredient, falafel is rich in protein and fiber. Falafel is also low in fat, cholesterol, and sodium; the key nutrients are calcium, iron, magnesium, phosphorus, zinc, copper, manganese, Vitamin C, Vitamin Thiamine and foliate.
In the vegetarian dish category, falafel is hearty enough to replace hamburger patties and meatballs.

GARBANZO BEANS STEW (fattet hummus bsamneh)

INGREDIENTS:

1 pita bread (toasted and broken into pieces)
1 batch hummus m'sabaha (see salad and spread chapter)
3 garlic cloves mashed with 1 tsp. salt
15.5 oz. cooked garbanzo beans, 3 cups of garbanzo broth
¼ cup pignoli nuts, ¼ cup I Can't Believe It's Not Butter! ®

PREPARATION:

To cook dried garbanzo beans, rinse one pound of the dried garbanzo beans and place in a three quart pot then mix in one tablespoon carbonated soda powder and set aside for about an hour. Cover the garbanzo beans with water and let them soak overnight. Bring the garbanzo beans to a boil, reduce the heat to medium and cook until they get soft and tender. Skim the froth from time to time. Place the toasted pita bread chips in a large serving bowl. Add one cup of the broth, the garlic, and 15.5 oz. cooked garbanzo beans and toss. Add another two cups of the hot broth; spread the hummus paste (m'sabaha) on the top. Fry the pignoli nuts with butter until they get golden brown. Spread the pignoli nuts and the hot butter on top of the hummus.
Serve hot next to a sliced sweet onion and pickles.
If pomegranate is in season, use some seeds of the pomegranate to garnish. (See picture)

SERVING SIZE: one cup
TOTAL SERVINGS: six

AMOUNT PER SERVING:

Calories	297.91 kcal
Total fat	18.33 g
Cholesterol	0.00 mg
Sodium	751.03 mg
Total carbohydrate	28.72 g
Dietary fiber	5.05 g
Protein	12.67 g

NOTE:

In the Middle East, especially in Damascus, this meal is served as a breakfast. Also you can use a can of garbanzo beans by opening the can, rinsing the garbanzo beans then adding fresh water and boiling them for half an hour. In this simplified way, you can use the beans and the broth for the meal.

GREEN FAVA BEAN STEW (fool m'taataa bil zait)

INGREDIENTS:

2 lbs. fresh fava beans (the inside beans only and the small tender pods with the skin)
1 cup chopped fresh cilantro, 4 cloves mashed garlic with 1 tsp. salt
½ cup olive oil, 2 tbsp. lemon juice (optional)

COOKING:

Sauté the cilantro and the garlic with two tbsp. of olive oil for about one minute then set aside.
Wash the pods, split them open and remove the beans, discard the pod skins that are not tender.
Heat the rest of the oil on high heat then add the beans and sauté until the skin of the bean is soft and tender, about 15-20 min. Add some hot water if needed.
Reduce the heat to low, then stir in the cilantro mixture.
Cook for about ten minutes more then add the lemon juice.
Serve with pita bread at room temperature.

SERVING SIZE: one ounce
TOTAL SERVINGS: twenty

AMOUNT PER SERVING:

Calories	43.20 kcal
Total fat	2.82 g
Cholesterol	0.00 mg
Sodium	98.20 mg
Total carbohydrate	3.00 g
Dietary fiber	2.06 g
Protein	1.43 g

NOTE:

Fava beans are rich in L-dopa, a substance used medically in the treatment of Parkinson's disease.
L-dopa is also a natriuretic agent which might help in controlling hypertension.
Green fava beans in cans may also be purchased at Middle Eastern grocery stores.

HARICOT BEANS (loubieh bil zait)

INGREDIENTS:
1 ½ lb. of haricot beans (loubieh) washed and cut up
1 medium size onion (chopped)
5 diced garlic cloves
¼ cup olive oil
1 tsp. salt
½ tsp. allspice

COOOKING:
On medium heat sauté onion, garlic, the beans, salt, and allspice with the oil. During sautéing, you may need to add a little water if needed.
Cook the meal on low heat for 15 to 20 minutes or until the loubieh become tender and well done.

SERVING SIZE: ½ cup
TOTAL SERVINGS: eight

AMOUNT PER SERVING:

Calories	101.00 kcal
Total fat	7.07 g
Cholesterol	0.00 mg
Sodium	3.69 mg
Total carbohydrate	10.03 g
Dietary fiber	1.90 g
Protein	2.12 g

NOTE:
This meal is delicious to be served with fried eggplant and pita bread.
Haricot beans are a good source of protein. The beans contain high amounts of calcium and iron.
They are low in saturated fat and sodium.
The benefit of the haricot beans can reduce intestinal problems, lower cholesterol and control blood pressure.

LENTILS AND RICE (m'jadara)

INGREDIENTS:

1 cup lentils (rinsed in cold water)
1 cup Uncle Ben's rice
4 cups of water, 1 small onion (chopped)
1 onion (slivered), 1/3 of cup olive oil
1 tsp. salt, 1 tsp. allspice

COOKING:

In a medium size pot, combine lentils, two cups of water, allspice and the chopped onion and bring to a boil then cover the pot and cook on low heat for half an hour or until the lentils are soft and the water is evaporated. In another pot, combine two cups of water, rice and the salt and bring to a boil then cook covered on low heat for half an hour. In the meantime fry the slivered onion in the oil until golden brown and crisp, then remove the onion from the oil and set aside.

When the process of cooking is finished, combine the lentils and rice and the hot oil and mix all together. Place the m'jadara in a serving plate and garnish with the crispy fried onion.

SERVING SIZE: one cup
TOTAL SERVINGS: seven

AMOUNT PER SERVING:	
Calories	85.65 kcal
Total fat	0.05 g
Cholesterol	0.00 mg
Sodium	400.70 mg
Total carbohydrate	17.58 g
Dietary Fiber	2.83 g
Protein	3.73 g

NOTE:

Enjoy with cabbage salad, yogurt and cucumber, plain yogurt or Middle Eastern salad.

There are different kinds of lentils: brown, red, and green. Brown lentils are used in the m'jadara. Lentils contain a high level of protein including essential amino acids. Also lentils are one of the best vegetable sources of iron. Some of the different lentil products require more cooking than others. Taste the lentils before you mix with the rice; if they are still not tender, add some water and cook a little longer.

LIMA BEANS (fasoulieh hab baida)

INGREDIENTS:

1 lb. large dried lima beans or five cups ready cooked frozen or from cans
½ cup olive oil, 1 sliced onion
2 14.5 ounce cans Italian or Mexican style stewed tomatoes (dice the large pieces)
4 cloves sliced garlic
¼ cup diluted tomato paste with 1 cup water, 1 tsp. salt

COOKING:

If you use dried beans rinse and remove the damaged pieces.
Soak the beans in 6 cups of cold water overnight.
Drain and replace the water with 6 cups of hot water.
Simmer gently on low heat with the lid tilted for thirty minutes or until the beans are tender.
Drain the water from the beans and set aside.
In a large sauce pan, sauté the onion with the olive oil until the onion is opaque and tender.
Add to the pan the lima beans, tomatoes, tomato paste, garlic, water and salt.
Bring to a boil, then reduce the heat to medium and simmer for 20 minutes or until the sauce thickens a bit.

SERVING SIZE: one cup
TOTAL SERVINGS: seven

AMOUNT PER SERVING:

Calories	261.73 kcal
Total fat	16.07 g
Cholesterol	0.00 mg
Sodium	693.36 mg
Total carbohydrate	41.37 g
Dietary fiber	13.20 g
Protein	12.47 g

NOTE:

You can add chopped celery and carrots to the ingredients (optional)
Enjoy with Arabic pita bread.

MAKING YOGURT (Laban)

INGREDIENTS:
½ gallon whole milk
¼ cup plain yogurt

MAKING:
Pour the milk into an eight quart pot and bring to a boil.
Shut off the heat; remove the pot from the stove top and let it cool to the point that you can put your finger into the milk, count to ten and tolerate the heat.
Mix the plain yogurt with the milk and cover the pot. Wrap the pot with a double folded blanket. Set aside to cool at least five hours or overnight.
When the mixture cools, the yogurt will be thickened. Transfer to a proper container and refrigerate.

SERVING SIZE: half cup
TOTAL SERVINGS: sixteen

AMOUNT PER SERVING:

Calories	90.00 kcal
Total fat	4.00 g
Cholesterol	17.50 mg
Sodium	80.00 mg
Total carbohydrate	8.55 g
Dietary fiber	0.00 g
Protein	5.50 g

NOTE:
Yogurt was introduced in Turkey, Eastern Europe, Western Asia, the Balkans, Russia, India and the Middle East.
People started making and eating yogurt since ancient times. The yogurt production started in the United States by an American couple – Sarkis and Rose Colombian and became popular in the 1950/1960's. The name of yogurt in Turkish is "yog~urt", in Arabic it is "laban", in Bulgarian it is "kselomlyako" and in Canada – "yoghurt".
The unique health benefits of yogurt are: rich in protein, calcium, riboflavin, Vitamin B_6 and VitaminB_{12}. Yogurt is also believed to promote good gum health.

MEATLESS STUFFING (hashweh syamee)

INGREDIENTS:
2 cups chopped parsley, 1 cup rice (rinsed)
1 cup chopped fine onion, 1 can garbanzo beans
1 cup chopped walnuts, ¼ cup lemon juice
1/8 cup pomegranate syrup
1 tsp. salt, 1 tsp. allspice
1/4 cup olive oil
1 fresh hard tomato (chopped fine)
Pinch of cayenne pepper (optional)

MIXING:
Rinse and drain the garbanzo beans.
Rinse the parsley and chop roughly.
In a large bowl, mix all the ingredients together.
This mixture can be used for stuffing grape leaf rolls, Swiss chard rolls, cabbage rolls, squash, and eggplants, etc.

SERVING SIZE: eight cups
TOTAL SERVINGS: eight cups

AMOUNT PER SERVING:

Calories	2143.10 kcal
Total fat	179.74 g
Cholesterol	0.00 mg
Sodium	5285.75 mg
Total carbohydrate	208.52 g
Dietary fiber	29.35 g
Protein	58.80 g

NOTE:
The stuffing is very healthy: you have the vegetables, the rice for carbohydrate and the garbanzo for protein. Also, the olive oil contains healthy fat and zero cholesterol.
The amounts of the ingredients are flexible; you can add more oil or rice or reduce the amount of parsley, and after you cook the first meal you will fix the hashweh to your desire.

OKRA STEW (bamya bil zait)

INGREDIENTS:
1 lb. fresh okra
1 cup chopped fresh cilantro
3 mashed garlic cloves
¼ cup olive oil
1 (14.5) oz. can Italian or Mexican stewed tomatoes
1/8 cup lemon juice (optional)
½ tsp. salt
½ tsp. allspice

COOKING:
Wash the okra very well, and then spread it out on a clean material to dry.
Clip the crown off each pod.
Fry the okra with the oil until golden brown, and then add salt, allspice, garlic and cilantro and sauté for five minutes.
Add the stewed tomatoes (chop the large pieces) and simmer on low heat for 20 minutes or until the okra is tender.
Remove from stovetop and add lemon juice if desired.

SERVING SIZE: half cup
TOTAL SERVINGS: eight

AMOUNT PER SERVING:

Calories	84.35 kcal
Total fat	6.89 g
Cholesterol	0.00 mg
Sodium	269.85 mg
Total carbohydrate	8.45 g
Dietary fiber	2.75 g
Protein	7.90 g

NOTE:
Also, you can use tomato sauce or tomato paste; use your judgment for the amount.
Serve at room temperature with pita bread.

PEA STEW (bazaila bil zait)

INGREDIENTS:

2 lbs. rinsed frozen or fresh peas
¼ cup olive oil
1 large chopped onion
6 sliced cloves garlic
1 can (14.5 oz.) Italian or Mexican style stewed tomatoes
3 oz. tomato paste
1 diced fresh tomato (8 oz.)
2 tsp. salt, 1 tsp. allspice, 4 cups water

COOKING:

With the oil, sauté garlic, onion with the salt and allspice until the onion is translucent and tender.
Add ½ cup hot water and the peas; cover the pot and cook on medium heat for about 15 minutes.
Dilute the tomato paste with the rest of the water and add to the pot.
Add the stewed tomatoes and the fresh tomato and cook on medium heat for 30 minutes or until the peas are tender.
Serve hot next to rice pilaf.

SERVING SIZE: one cup
TOTAL SERVINGS: thirteen

AMOUNT PER SERVING:

Calories	103.54 kcal
Total fat	4.24 g
Cholesterol	0.00 mg
Sodium	589.17 mg
Total carbohydrate	14.85 g
Dietary fiber	4.35 g
Protein	4.79 g

NOTE:

Peas contain Vitamin A, Vitamin B, and Vitamin C, beta-carotene, thiamin, riboflavin, niacin, iron, magnesium, phosphorus, potassium and zinc.

RICE PILAF (riz m'falfal)

INGREDIENTS:
1 cup Uncle Ben's rice
2 cups water
1/4 cup I Can't Believe It's Not Butter!®
1 tbsp. vermicelli (sh'airieh)
1/2 tsp. salt

COOKING:
Sauté the vermicelli with the butter until it becomes golden brown.
Add the rest of the ingredients and bring to a boil.
Reduce the heat to low and cover the pot.
Cook the rice for one half hour, or until the water is completely evaporated.
Serve hot next to stew meals, or with plain yogurt spread on the top of the rice.

SERVING SIZE: half cup
TOTAL SERVINGS: six

AMOUNT PER SERVING:

Calories	41.83 kcal
Total fat	6.75 g
Cholesterol	0.00 mg
Sodium	194.00 mg
Carbohydrate	2.81 g
Dietary Fiber	0.16 g
Protein	0.77 g

NOTE:
Rice is high in potassium, phosphorus and calcium.
Also rice contains zinc, manganese and iron.
In the Middle East, rice is served next to almost every stew meal.
You can use the same method of cooking rice pilaf for cooking (bulgur pilaf).

ROLLED SWISS CHARD (selik malfoof)

INGREDIENTS:
Two bunches of green Swiss chard washed (about 2 lbs.)
One recipe of meatless stuffing
(Look for "meatless stuffing" in this chapter.)
¼ cup lemon juice

COOKING:
Cut out the stems of the Swiss chard and set aside.
Cut the large leaves into large grape leaf size; spread the Swiss chard out on clean material to soften overnight (see Note). Place one leaf on a serving plate; add one tablespoon of the stuffing. Gather the stuffing with your fingers along the edge of the leaf facing your body.
Fold the right and the left edges over the stuffing and roll the leaf. (See stuffed grape leaves in this chapter). Cover the inside bottom of a three quart pot or larger with some damaged leaves. Place all the rolled leaves in the pot and cover with a plate and a weight over it so that when you add the water to the pot the rolls won't float to the surface. Add water to the pot to the level of the plate,
Bring to a boil; then reduce the heat to low and cook for one hour. Remove from the stove and remove the plate and weight. Add the lemon juice and swivel the pot around for the juice to mix thoroughly. During cooking, add more hot water to the pot if the broth dries out considerably.
Let the rolls cool then drain the liquid. Serve with pita bread at room temperature.

SERVING SIZE: one rolled leaf
TOTAL SERVINGS: twenty six

AMOUNT PER SERVING:

Calories	74.00 kcal
Total fat	5.48 g
Cholesterol	0.00 mg
Sodium	145.87 mg
Total carbohydrate	5.73 g
Fiber	1.30 g
Protein	1.96 g

NOTE:
A-before you roll the leaves, spread them out on a table overnight to dry out and get soft.
B-cut up the stems to half inch size and boil, then let cool and freeze for future recipes.

SPINACH WITH OIL (khibeizeh)

INGREDIENTS:
2½ lbs. fresh baby leaf spinach (chopped)
1 large onion (slivered), ¼ cup olive oil
4 cloves garlic mashed with 1 tsp. salt

COOKING:
Wash the spinach thoroughly.
Boil the spinach about 15 minutes or until it becomes soft.
Drain the water from the pot.
Place the spinach in a strainer.
Place the strainer under the faucet and rinse the spinach with cold water.
Squeeze the water completely from the spinach with your hands and place them in a serving plate.
Fry the slivered onion with olive oil until the slivers become crispy or light brown.
Remove the fried onion from the oil and set aside.
Sauté the garlic with ¼ cup of the remaining hot oil; add the oil and the garlic to the spinach and mix together.
Garnish with the slivered onion and serve.

SERVING SIZE: half cup
TOTAL SERVINGS: six

AMOUNT PER SERVING:
Calories	130.39 kcal
Total fat	9.40 g
Cholesterol	0.00 mg
Sodium	488.76 mg
Total carbohydrate	9.58 g
Dietary fiber	15.15 g
Protein	4.87 g

NOTE:
Spinach has high nutritional value and is extremely rich in antioxidants.
It is a rich source of Vitamin A, (especially high in lutien), Vitamin C, Vitamin E, Vitamin K, magnesium, manganese, folate, selenium, and omega 3 fatty acid. Spinach is considered to be a rich source of iron. Also, spinach is high in calcium.
Stuff khibeizeh in pocket pita bread; add a squeeze of fresh lemon and enjoy.

SQUASH WITH LEMON (kousa b'hamod)

INGREDIENTS:

2 ½ pounds Mexican squash (cleaned and cut to about one inch cubes)
1 medium size onion (slivered)
1 tsp. salt, ¼ cup oil
1 tsp. dried crushed mint leaves
6 cloves garlic (mashed), ¼ cup lemon juice

COOKING:

Sauté the onion with salt and oil until the onion becomes opaque.
Add the squash and cook on medium heat setting for about 20 minutes.
Add the mint leaves, garlic and lemon juice and cook for five more minutes.
Enjoy at room temperature with pita bread.

SERVING SIZE: half cup
TOTAL SERVINGS: eight

AMOUNT PER SERVING:

Calories	103.00 kcal
Total fat	7.00 g
Cholesterol	0.00 mg
Sodium	293.00 mg
Total carbohydrate	10.00 g
Dietary fiber	3.00 g
Protein	2.00 g

NOTE:

Botanically, the squash is considered a fruit.
Squash can be served fresh in salad or with meatless stuffing, fried, barbecued, and many other dishes as you see in different categories of this book.
Also, small squash can be pickled.
Squash contain protein, riboflavin (Vitamin B2), Vitamin C, and potassium.

STRING BEAN STEW (fasoulieh b'zait)

INGREDIENTS:
2 lbs. fresh string beans (washed & cut)
1 cup chopped onion
1/3 cup olive oil
6 cloves garlic
1 tsp. salt
½ tsp. allspice
15 oz. can tomato sauce

COOKING:
In a three quart pot, place all the ingredients except tomato sauce and garlic.
Sauté for ten minutes then add 1/2 cup water and simmer for 15 minutes on medium heat.
Add tomato sauce, two cups water and the garlic, cover and cook on low heat for one-half hour or until the string beans are tender.
Serve hot next to rice pilaf or at room temperature with pita bread.

SERVING SIZE: one cup
TOTAL SERVINGS: seven

AMOUNT PER SERVING:
Calories	17.00 kcal
Total fat	10.80 g
Cholesterol	0.00 mg
Sodium	531.00 mg
Total carbohydrate	17.20 g
Dietary fiber	5.60 g
Protein	4.10 g

NOTE:
String beans are high in potassium and contain Vitamin C.
You can substitute the tomato sauce with Italian style stewed tomatoes, Mexican style stewed tomatoes or simply with freshly ripened tomatoes.

STUFFED ARTICHOKE HEARTS (ardishokee)

INGREDIENTS:

1 lb. artichoke hearts (frozen or from the jar)
1 cup chopped onion, 1 cup peas, and 1 cup chopped carrots
5 cloves garlic (mashed with a little salt)
½ cup olive oil, 1 tsp. salt, 1 tsp. allspice
2 ½ cups warmed water, 1/8 cup lemon juice

COOKING:

In a large pan, heat the oil on medium heat; add the onion, salt and allspice and cook until the onions are opaque and tender. Add to the pan the peas, carrots, crushed garlic and sauté for five minutes. Remove the mixture from the pan and set aside.

Place the artichoke hearts around the inside edges of the pan.

Add the peas and the carrot mixture to fill the artichoke hearts and place the rest of the mixture into the center of the pan (see picture).

Add the warmed water, cover the pan and simmer on low heat for forty-five minutes to one hour or until the artichokes are tender and can be easily cut with a fork.

Take out the artichokes and lay them on a serving platter and add lemon juice. Serve at room temperature with Arabic pita bread.

SERVING SIZE: one artichoke with ½ cup stuffing
TOTAL SERVINGS: ten

_____

AMOUNT PER SERVING:

Calories	155.04 kcal
Total fat	10.99 g
Cholesterol	0.00 mg
Sodium	308.38 mg
Total carbohydrate	13.24 g
Dietary fiber	4.57 g
Protein	3.16 g

NOTE:

If you use fresh artichoke hearts, make sure to boil them first.

The artichoke has a nutritional value that aids digestion and strengthens liver function and the gall bladder. Artichokes also raise HDL/LDL ratios and reduce cholesterol levels.

STUFFED EGGPLANTS (baitinjan mihshee)

INGREDIENTS:

12 medium size eggplants, half a recipe of meatless stuffing
1 tbsp. dried mint leaves crumbled, 1 tsp. salt, 1 can tomato sauce (15 oz.)
5 cloves garlic (sliced)

COOKING:

Wash the eggplants very well. Snip the tops of the eggplant to have a flat area about ¾ an inch.
Then carefully core (*) the eggplant, taking out the inside and discard. Now, dissolve ½ tsp. salt with ¼ cup water
and pour it into one of the eggplants, cover the opening of that eggplant with your thumb and shake the liquid
inside. Transfer the liquid from one to the other until you do all of them; then throw out the remaining liquid. With a
knife, slit the bottom of each eggplant in the shape of a small **x** large enough to allow air to escape when you stuff
the eggplant. Stuff the eggplant with the meatless stuffing and place them in an eight quart pot. Add tomato sauce,
garlic, mint leaves and water to cover the eggplants. On a high heat setting, bring to a boil then reduce the heat to
low. Cover the pot and cook for one hour or until the eggplants are soft and tender.

SERVING SIZE: one eggplant with ½ cup sauce
TOTAL SERVINGS: twelve

AMOUNT PER SERVING:

Calories	118.27 kcal
Total fat	7.67 g
Cholesterol	0.00 mg
Sodium	540.25 mg
Total carbohydrate	15.61 g
Dietary fiber	1.94 g
Protein	3.42 g

NOTE:

*A special corer for removing the eggplant centers is available at Middle Eastern grocery stores.
You can freeze the cooked eggplant by wrapping each one individually with plastic wrap and then in a plastic freezer
bags before you place them in the freezer.
Also you can freeze the broth separately in a container.

STUFFED GRAPE LEAVES (yabraa syamee)

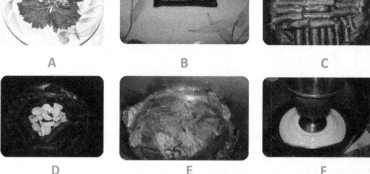

INGREDIENTS:
70 fresh, frozen or pickled (in a jar) grape leaves
1 batch meatless stuffing (see meatless stuffing)
1/8 cup lemon juice, 6 cloves garlic (slivered)

PREPARATION:
Place a flat serving plate on the table. Lay one grape leaf flat on the plate.
Take one tablespoon of the mixture and place it on the grape leaf, (see figure A).
Fold the two sides of the grape leaf over the stuffing, and then fold the top end of the leaf that facing your body over, and with your thumbs and fingers, start rolling the leaf (B).
In a large pot, lay five or more plain grapes leaves over the inside bottom of the pot.
Place the rolled grape leaves in the pot. (C)
Place the garlic on the top of the grape leaves (D).
Cover with more leaves (E).
Place over the grape leaves a large plate and place a weight over it (F).
Add water to the pot up to the plate level. Bring to a boil.
Reduce the heat to low and cook for ninety minutes or until the grape leaves are tender.
Turn off the heat; add the lemon juice and let rest for about fifteen minutes then remove
The weight and plate and place the grape leaves on a serving platter.

SERVING SIZE: one
TOTAL SERVINGS: sixty

AMOUNT PER SERVING:

Calories	39.05 kcal
Total fat	3.05 g
Cholesterol	0.00 mg
Sodium	54.84 mg
Total carbohydrate	4.07 g
Dietary Fiber	0.79 g
Protein	1.16 g

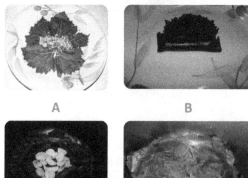

A   B   C

D   E   F

NOTE:
Stuffed grape leaves can be frozen by placing in a tight container.
Serve at room temperature next to pita bread.

STUFFED SQUASH (kousa syamee)

INGREDIENTS:
12 medium size Mexican squash, 6 garlic cloves (slivered), meatless stuffing (see meatless stuffing)
2 tbsp. olive oil, 1 tbsp. dried, crushed mint leaves; water.

COOKING:
Wash the squash very well. Clip the top of the squash to have a flat area about ¾" and scrape the dry thin area at the bottom of the squash, and then carefully core (*) the squash taking out the pulp and discard. Now dissolve ½ tsp. salt with ¼ cup water and pour it into one squash, cover the top of that squash with your thumb and shake the liquid inside. Then transfer the liquid one to the other until you do all of them. Dispose any liquid that remains. With a knife, slit the bottom of each squash into the shape of a small **x** big enough to allow the air to escape when you stuff the squash. Stuff the squash densely by pushing the stuffing inside the squash with your finger, then place the squash in a large pot and add water to cover the squash; also, add olive oil, mint leaves and garlic. Bring to a boil then reduce the heat to low and cook for one hour or until the squash are done. Serve at room temperature.

SERVING SIZE: one squash
TOTAL SERVINGS: twelve

AMOUNT PER SERVING:

Calories	196.79 kcal
Total fat	15.49 g
Cholesterol	0.00 mg
Sodium	713.92 mg
Total carbohydrate	18.43 g
Dietary fiber	2.97 g
Protein	5.63 g

NOTE:
(*)You can purchase a corer (maawara) at any Middle Eastern grocery store.
You can freeze the cooked squash by wrapping each one individually with plastic wrap then in freezer plastic bags. Also you can freeze the leftover cooking liquid separately in a container.
Squash is considered a vegetable but botanically speaking squash is a fruit. You can eat it raw or cut up in a salad.

SWISS CHARD WITH SESAME SEED PASTE (selik bil tahineh)

INGREDIENTS:
½ lb. fresh Swiss chard or frozen stems (see note at stuffed Swiss chard)
¼ cup sesame seed paste (tahineh)
1/8 cup lemon juice
1/8 cup water
1/8 cup low fat yogurt
½ tsp. salt
4 cloves garlic mashed with the salt

COOKING:
Wash the Swiss chard thoroughly and cut the leaves into strips; then cut the leaves and the stems into half inch pieces.
Boil the chard for about half an hour or until the stems becomes soft and translucent.
Move the pot to the sink and open cold water onto the pot to stop the process of cooking.
Drain well and set aside.
In a serving bowl, mix the mashed garlic, sesame seed paste, water, lemon juice and the yogurt.
Add the Swiss chard to the paste mixture and stir lightly.
Serve at room temperature with Arabic pita bread.

SERVING SIZE: one ounce
TOTAL SERVINGS: twelve

AMOUNT PER SERVING:

Calories	36.20 kcal
Total fat	24.05 g
Cholesterol	0.15 mg
Sodium	138.13 mg
Total carbohydrate	2.86 g
Dietary fiber	0.92 g
Protein	1.47 g

NOTE:
Swiss chard is high in Vitamins K and C.
It is also rich in minerals, dietary fiber and protein.

VEGETABLE STEW (kawaj)

INGREDIENTS:

1 eggplant about 14 oz. peeled and cut into about one inch cubes
1 squash about 14 oz. cut into one inch pieces
2 potatoes about 18 oz. peeled and cut into one inch pieces
2 onions about 14 oz. peeled and slivered
1/4 cup olive oil (*)
1 can Italian or Mexican style stewed tomatoes
1 can ready cut tomatoes
Salt and pepper to taste

BAKING:

In a 9" x 13" roasting pan, mix all the ingredients except the tomatoes; then place under the broiler until the vegetables become golden brown; remove occasionally and stir vegetables to evenly brown.
Add the tomatoes and one cup water.
Bake the stew in a pre-heated oven at 350 degrees for 45 minutes or until the meal is done.
You may need to add more water if required.
Serve hot with rice pilaf.

SERVING SIZE: one cup
TOTAL SERVINGS: six

AMOUNT PER SERVING:

Calories	181.78 kcal
Total fat	10.44 g
Cholesterol	0.00 mg
Sodium	566 .46 mg
Total carbohydrate	34.47 g
Dietary Fiber	7.41 g
Protein	4.50 g

NOTE:

(*)If you wish a richer flavor, add another ¼ cup olive oil.
Vegetable stew is a favorite vegetarian Middle Eastern meal.
It is tasty, low in calories with zero cholesterol.

WHITE CHEESE (jibneh baida)

INGREDIENTS:
1 gallon reduced fat two percent milk
¼ tablet rennet
Or 1 tbsp. liquid rennet

MAKING CHEESE:
Place the milk in a large pot.
Dissolve the rennet in 1 tbsp. water and add to the milk or add the liquid (rennet).
Place the pot on medium heat and constantly stir until the milk curdles.
Pour the mixture into cheesecloth and save the drained liquid for future use if desired.
Collect the cheese from the cloth with your hands, form a ball and refrigerate.
If you have a mesh yogurt strainer, place the cheese ball in it and press down and refrigerate.

SERVING SIZE: one ounce
TOTAL SERVINGS: twenty

_____

AMOUNT PER SERVING:

Calories	106.00 kcal
Total fat	8.50 g
Cholesterol	30.00 mg
Sodium	321.00 mg
Total carbohydrate	1.30 g
Dietary fiber	0.00 g
Protein	6.80 g

NOTE:
The next day if you see more liquid drain out of the cheese, discard the liquid. Place the cheese in salted water.
Cheese supplies a great deal of calcium, protein, phosphorus and fat. Cheese is usually made from milk of cows, goats or sheep. Cheese is an ancient food originated most likely in the Middle East.
The origin of cheese making ranges from 8000 BCE to around 3000 BCE, when the sheep were first domesticated and the first cheese may have been made by the people of the Middle East or Central Asia.
The earliest archeological evidence of cheese making has been found in Egyptian tomb murals 2000 BCE.

WHEAT (ameh)

INGREDIENTS:

1 cup skinless whole wheat kernels (8 oz.)
½ cup crushed walnuts
¼ cup sugar, ½ tsp. cinnamon
½ cup golden raisins
½ tsp. ground anise
1 cup candied almonds

COOKING:

Rinse the wheat in cold water.
Place in a cooking pot; cover with water and soak overnight or at least for eight hours.
Then replace the water with fresh water and cook on medium heat for 45 minutes to two hours (depends on the brand of the wheat) or until the wheat is thoroughly softened.
Drain and rinse with cold water.
Spread the wheat over a clean sheet of material to dry about eight hours.
When the wheat is dry, place it in a bowl and mix it with the rest of the ingredients.

SERVING SIZE: one cup
TOTAL SERVINGS: seven

AMOUNT PER SERVING:

Calories	188.20 kcal
Total fat	5.60 g
Cholesterol	0.00 mg
Sodium	1.70 mg
Total carbohydrate	38.70 g
Dietary Fiber	31.80 g
Protein	37.60 g

NOTE:

Serve warm for breakfast or as a snack. In the Christian Eastern Rite faith, ameh is served in the church as a food of mercy in this fashion. Place the mixture in a flat round tray and form it into a heap. Cover with plastic wrap and with your palms press down so that the ameh becomes firm. Remove the plastic and discard it. Cover the top with powdered sugar (optional), and then decorate the shape of a cross in the center with candy coated white almonds and the rest of the surface with silver dragees (optional). Place a candle in the center.

PASTRIES AND SWEETS

ANISE COOKIES (kaak yansoon)

INGREDIENTS:

1 cup I Can't Believe It's Not Butter! ®
1 cup sugar
¾ cup eggbeaters
4 cups flour
2 tsp. baking powder
½ tsp. salt
1/8 cup ground anise seeds
1/8 cup anise seeds

BAKING:

In a mixing bowl cream the eggbeaters, butter and sugar. Then add the rest of the ingredients.
Mix and knead very well to create a bread dough consistency. Divide the dough into thirty-six pieces the size of a walnut (1/8 of a cup). Roll each piece between your palms creating snake shapes about 3" to 4" long. Fold one end over the other to have a donut shape. Place cookies on a greased baking tray and place the tray in a preheated oven at 375 degrees on the center rack. Bake for 25 minutes or until light golden brown. Remove from the oven and set aside to cool. Enjoy the kaak as a snack with tea or with a cup of Turkish coffee.

SERVING SIZE: one
TOTAL SERVINGS: thirty six

AMOUNT PER SERVING:

Calories	111.35 kcal
Total fat	4.56 g
Cholesterol	0.00 mg
Sodium	39.02 mg
Total carbohydrate	15.94 g
Dietary Fiber	0.56 g
Protein	0.96 g

NOTE:

These cookies are a wonderful choice for breakfast or afternoon tea; they are satisfying as a pastry cookie but are not overly sweet. The anise flavoring makes them distinctive.

BAKED SEMOLINA TRAY (hareesa or nammora)

INGREDIENTS:

4 cups smeed (semolina), 1-1/4 cup rendered butter
1 cup sugar, ½ tsp. baking soda
2 tsp. baking powder, dash of salt
1-1/2 cups plain yogurt, 2 tbsp. yogurt
40 blanched almonds, 3 cups attir (syrup)
1 tbsp. tahineh paste

BAKING:

A- Mix smeed, butter and sugar and set aside for 3 to 4 hours. B- Stir baking powder, baking soda and salt into the yogurt. C- Grease a 13"x17" baking tray with tahineh. Mix A and B and spread the mixture evenly into the tray. Smooth the top with the 2 tbsp. of yogurt, using a spatula, then score the top (which you will cut after baking) to equal 40 squares. Push a piece of almond in the center of every square. Preheat the oven to 350 degrees and bake for 45 minutes or until the top is golden brown.
Take it out of the oven and set it aside to cool. With a knife cut the scored line then pour the attir (syrup). (See sugar/syrup recipe.)

SERVING SIZE: one square
TOTAL SERVINGS: forty

AMOUNT PER SERVING:

Calories	204.23 kcal
Total fat	7.23 g
Cholesterol	16.09 mg
Sodium	23.45 mg
Total carbohydrate	26.33 g
Dietary fiber	1.90 g
Protein	3.17 g

NOTE:

Hareesa is one of the popular sweets in the Middle East; it is also called "nammora".
3.5 g of semolina contain 3.5 g dietary fiber, 12.68 g protein, 17 mg calcium, 1.23 mg iron, 47 mg magnesium, 136 mg phosphorus, and other vitamins.

BAKLAVA ROLLS (baklawa malfoof)

INGREDIENTS:
Dough: 1 lb. fillo dough, 3/4 cup I Can't Believe It's Not Butter!®
Stuffing: 2 cups crushed fine walnuts
 1 tsp. ground cinnamon, 1/2 tsp. ground nutmeg
 ½ cup sugar, 1/8 cup orange blossom water
Dipping: one cup sugar syrup (attir), ¼ tsp. ground cloves
Garnish: 1/8 cup ground pistachio nuts

BAKING:

Mix the walnuts, 1/8 cup I Can't Believe It's Not Butter!®, cinnamon, nutmeg, cloves, sugar and orange blossom water and set aside; this should measure twenty-seven tablespoons. Melt the rest of the butter and set aside. Open the fillo dough box and lay the sheets flat on the counter and Cover with a damp linen cloth; this is to keep the fillo dough from drying. Take one sheet of the dough, fold it in half, and then brush it with butter. Take one tablespoon of the mixture and lay it on the folded sheet (see figure A) then fold the two ends over to meet in the center and brush them with butter (figure B); then start rolling (figure C) and lay the rolled seam side down in a baking tray and brush with butter; repeating the process until you finish all of them. Bake in a preheated oven at 350 degrees for fifty minutes or until golden. Take the tray out of the oven and pour the attir over all and garnish with the pistachio nuts. Serve at room temperature.

SERVING SIZE: one roll
TOTAL SERVINGS: twenty seven

_____

AMOUNT PER SERVING:

Calories	176.29 kcal
Total fat	9.87 g
Cholesterol	0.00 mg
Sodium	110.27 mg
Total carbohydrate	20.13 g
Dietary fiber	0.98 g
Protein	2.30 g

A   B   C

NOTE:
You can substitute walnuts with crushed pistachio nuts.
Also, the roll would be richer in taste if you use rendered butter instead of I Can't Believe It's Not Butter!® if you are not considering cholesterol.

BAKLAVA TRAY WITH NUTS (baklawa)

INGREDIENTS:
2 lbs. fillo dough
1 lb. chopped walnuts
2 cups sweet rendered butter (see recipe for rendered butter)
½ tsp. ground nutmeg, ½ tsp. ground cinnamon
1 tbsp. sugar, 2 cups attir

BAKING:
Grease a 13"x17" baking tray with 2 tbsp. butter. Take one lb. of the fillo dough and unroll it in a baking tray. In a mixing bowl, mix the walnuts, nutmeg, cinnamon, sugar and two tbsp. of butter. Spread the nut mixture evenly on top of the fillo dough in the tray. Lay the other pound of the fillo on top of the mixture. With a sharp knife, cut through the dough to equal forty squares or triangles. Pour the rest of the melted butter on the top. Bake the baklava in a preheated oven at 375 degrees for about 1 ½ hours or until the top is golden brown. Cool the baklawa tray for about five minutes then pour the attir over the entire tray.

SERVING SIZE: one square
TOTAL SERVINGS: forty

AMOUNT PER SERVING:

Calories	244.51 kcal
Total fat	14.86 g
Cholesterol	24.80 mg
Sodium	161.80 mg
Total carbohydrate	24.45 g
Dietary fiber	1.52 g
Protein	4.04 g

NOTE:
Baklava, in Arabic"baklawa", is extremely popular in the Middle East, Turkey, Greece and around the world. You can substitute the walnuts with pistachio nuts.
The history of baklava is not well documented; many Ottoman sweets are similar to Byzantine sweets and that is what many believe the origin of baklava is, "Byzantium".
For less calories and much reduced cholesterol use I Can't Believe It's Not Butter!®.

CARDAMOM COOKIES (ka'ak hab el'hail)

INGREDIENTS:
1 cup I Can't Believe It's Not Butter!®
1 cup sugar
3/4 cup eggbeaters
4 cups flour
2 1/2 tsp. baking powder
1/2 tsp. salt
¼ of a cup ground cardamom

BAKING:
Cream the eggbeaters, butter and sugar.
In a separate bowl, mix the rest of the ingredients.
Gradually, add the mixture to the creamed eggbeaters and butter, knead very well to create a bread dough consistency. Divide the dough to 36 pieces the size of a walnut (1/8 of a cup) each.
Roll each piece between your palms creating snake shapes about 3" to 4" long.
Fold one end over the other to have a donut shaped cookie. Place on greased baking tray.
Bake in a preheated oven at 375 degrees on the middle rack for 25 minutes or until light golden brown.

SERVING SIZE: one
TOTAL SERVING: thirty four

AMOUNT PER SERVING:

Calories	117.31 kcal
Total fat	4.75 g
Cholesterol	0.00 mg
Sodium	41.32 mg
Total carbohydrate	16.95 g
Dietary Fiber	0.66 g
Protein	0.95 g

NOTE:
Cardamom has a strong unique taste, with an intensely aromatic fragrance.
A cardamom cookie is delicious with a cup of Arabic coffee.

CREAM OF RICE (mighlee)

INGREDIENTS:

1 cup ground rice powder, 1/2 cup sugar
8 cups water, 2 tbsp. ground caraway
1 tsp. cinnamon, 1/4 cup almond halves
1/8 cup pignoli nuts, 1/8cup pistachio nuts
1/8 cup shredded coconut (optional)

COOKING:

Place the rice, sugar, caraway and the cinnamon in a two quart pot and mix very well. Add the water, stir the mixture and bring to a boil.

Reduce the heat to low; cover the pot and cook for ten minutes. Uncover the pot and cook for another twenty minutes or until the mixture thickens stirring all the time.

Pour the mighlee into a large serving plate and garnish with the almonds, pistachios, pignoli nuts and coconut. Serve cold as a dessert.

SERVING SIZE: one cup
TOTAL SERVINGS: eight

AMOUNT PER SERVING:

Calories	94.10 kcal
Total fat	2.41 g
Cholesterol	0.00 mg
Sodium	1.03 mg
Total carbohydrate	24.30 g
Dietary fiber	1.49 g
Protein	3.05 g

NOTE:

English usage of the term "caraway' dates back to at least the year 1440 and is considered by Walter William Skeat (principals of English etymology) to be of Arabic origin: "El-caraway".

Rice powder is available at any Middle Eastern grocery store.

CRISP DOUGH BALLS (awwameh)

INGREDIENTS:

1 lb. flour, 1 packet yeast, ½ tsp. sugar
3 cups attir, 2 1/2 cups water
Dash of salt, oil for frying

PREPARING AND FRYING:

Dissolve the yeast with ¼ cup lukewarm water, sprinkle with ½ tsp. sugar, cover and let it rise.

In a mixing bowl, combine the flour, water, salt and the dissolved yeast and mix; cover and set aside to rise. Heat the oil in a deep frying pan.

Fill a soup bowl with water and place a soup spoon in it.

With the spoon, pick up some of the dough and drop it into the hot oil.

Place the spoon back in the water, take it out shake it and again pick up some dough and drop it into the hot oil. Fry one batch until golden brown.

Remove from the oil and place in the attir. While you are frying the next batch, remove the first batch from the attir and place in a serving platter. Repeat the process until you finish all.

Garnish with homemade cream (ishta) or with whipped cream. Serve hot or at room temperature.

SERVING SIZE: five balls
TOTAL SERVINGS: twenty

AMOUNT PER SERVING:

Calories	159.16 kcal
Total fat	8.16 g
Cholesterol	0.00 mg
Sodium	6.34 mg
Total carbohydrate	20.05 g
Dietary fiber	2.05 g
Protein	2.03 g

NOTE:

In Damascus, Syria, at a summer evening, people gather and play cards and they bet for awwameh. At the end of the evening, the loser goes out to the sweet shop and brings back the awwameh for all to share and they tease each other about the game.

FRIED DOUGH (zalabieh)

INGREDIENTS:

2 cups all-purpose flour (sifted)
1 tbsp. dry yeast or (one packet)
½ tsp. sugar
Dash of salt, powdered sugar
½ tsp. ground mahlab (black cherry kernels)
½ tsp. ground anise seeds
1 cup plus water
Oil for frying

PREPARING AND FRYING:

Dissolve the yeast in ¼ cup lukewarm water, sprinkle with the sugar, cover and set aside to rise.
In a mixing bowl or in a dough mixing machine, mix the flour, mahlab, ground anise seeds and the salt.
Then, add the yeast and gradually add the water while you are mixing.
Set aside for about thirty minutes for the dough to rise.
Divide the dough into balls the size of a walnut (1/8 of a cup) and set aside to rise for about twenty minutes. Fry the dough balls in hot oil until golden.
Remove from the oil and sprinkle with powdered sugar and serve.

SERVING SIZE: one ball
TOTAL SERVINGS: twenty four

AMOUNT PER SERVING:

Calories	54.80 kcal
Total fat	2.27 g
Cholesterol	0.00 mg
Sodium	1.28 mg
Total carbohydrate	92.81 g
Dietary fiber	0.44 g
Protein	0.44 g

NOTE:

During frying, make sure to flip the dough balls over to get them evenly browned.

PANCAKES WITH RICOTTA (atayef asafiri)

INGREDIENTS:
Pancake dough: 1 cup flour, 1 cup lukewarm water, dash of salt, 1 packet dry yeast or one tsp. dry yeast,
¼ cup lukewarm water, ¼ tsp. sugar
Stuffing: 1 lb. whole milk ricotta
Garnish: Sprinkle of cinnamon, ½ cup (attir) sugar syrup (look for the recipe in this Chapter); quince preserves (optional)

COOKING:
Dissolve the yeast with ¼ cup lukewarm water, sprinkle with the sugar and set aside to rise.
Place the flour, water, salt and the dissolved yeast in a dough mixing machine and knead on low speed then increase to high speed and knead for one minute. Place the mixture in a bowl, cover and set aside to rise for about forty minutes. Mix the dough with a spoon every fifteen minutes to prevent the dough from separating. Heat a pancake griddle well then drop one teaspoon of the mixture on the griddle.
Remove from the griddle when pores form on the surface of the pancake; place on a flat tray one next to another and set aside to cool.
Take one pancake in your left hand and pinch one end together then place one heaping teaspoon of ricotta in the middle of the pancake (see picture). Arrange all the fixed pancakes in a serving plate and sprinkle with cinnamon powder and place about ½ tsp. attir on each one.
Enjoy as a dessert.

SERVING SIZE: one
TOTAL SERVINGS: forty four

AMOUNT PER SERVING:

Calories	41.27 kcal
Total fat	1.19 g
Cholesterol	5.11 mg
Sodium	14.92 mg
Total carbohydrate	4.68 g
Dietary fiber	0.00 g
Protein	0.00 g

NOTE:
You can take a pinch of quince jam and place on the ricotta for decoration (optional).

PASTRY DOUGH STUFFED WITH ALMONDS (karabeej)

INGREDIENTS:

(Dough) 3 cups flour, 1 ¾ cups farina (smeed), 1 cup I Can't Believe It's Not Butter!®, dash of salt, 1½ tbsp. sugar, 1 cup milk, ¼ tsp. mahlab, ¼ tsp. Arabic gum, 1 tbsp. dry yeast, ¼ tsp. sugar

(Stuffing) 1 cup chopped almonds, ¼ tsp. ground cinnamon, 1/8 tsp. ground cloves, 1/8 tsp. ground nutmeg, and 1 tbsp. powdered sugar, 2 tbsp. I Can't Believe It's Not Butter!®

(Topping) marshmallow cream

PREPARING AND BAKING:

Mix the stuffing ingredients together by rubbing the mixture between your palms and set aside.

Mix the flour, farina, sugar, salt and butter by rubbing the mixture between your palms; cover and set aside for overnight or at least eight hours. Dissolve the yeast with ¼ cup lukewarm water, sprinkle with ¼ tsp. sugar and set aside to rise. Dissolve the Arabic gum and the mahlab with 1/8 cup cold water.

Add the gum, mahlab, the yeast and the milk to the flour mixture and mix well; don't knead. Cut the dough to pieces the size of ¼ cup and roll the pieces between your palms, then with your finger make a dent in the middle of the ball and shape it like a cup and fill it with stuffing. Close the dent and shape the ball like a blimp. Place the karabeej on a greased baking tray and place the tray on the top shelf in the oven, bake in a preheated oven at 400 degrees for twenty-five minutes or until light brown. Take the tray out of the oven, set aside to cool.

SERVING SIZE: one
TOTAL SERVINGS: thirty five

AMOUNT PER SERVING:

Calories	143.06 kcal
Total fat	7.15 g
Cholesterol	0.57 mg
Sodium	22.22 mg
Total carbohydrate	16.72 g
Dietary fiber	1.05 g
Protein	2.51 g

NOTE:

Dip the karabeej in the marshmallow cream and serve.

Marshmallow cream can be purchased from any supermarket around your neighborhood.

PASTRY DOUGH STUFFED WITH DATES (maamool ajweh)

INGREDIENTS:
Stuffing: 1 lb. and 6 oz. dates (ajweh), 4 tbsps. I Can't Believe It's Not Butter!®, ½ cup rosewater,
Dough: 3 lbs. and 5 oz. farina, 3 cups flour, 2 1/2 cups I Can't Believe It's Not Butter!®,1/4 tsp. mahlab, 1 cup sugar, ½ cup orange blossom water, 1 cup lukewarm water, 2 packets yeast, ½ tsp. sugar, 1 tsp. mahlab (black cherry kernel powder), wooden mold shaper.

BAKING:
Mix the yeast with ¼ cup lukewarm water, sprinkle with ¼ tsp. sugar and set aside to rise.
Place 4 tsp. butter in a pan and melt it on low heat. Add the dates and mix well with the butter, then set aside. Place farina, flour, sugar, and mahlab in a bowl and mix well. Add to the mixture the 2 ½ cups melted butter and rub the mixture with your hand to blend the butter with all the mixture. Add rosewater and the orange blossom water and the yeast and mix lightly with your fingers; don't knead. Cover and set aside for about five hours. Take a piece of the dough the size of a walnut, place it in your left hand palm and with your right hand index finger make a deep dent in the dough and press against your palm to make the dough like a cup. Fill the cup with a piece of the ajweh and gently close the dough over the ajweh, then place it in the wooden mold and press in gently to make the bottom of the maamool flat. Turn the mold upside down and hit it at the edge of the table to release the maamool and drop on your palm. Place all the maamool on a greased baking sheet and set aside for one hour. Bake in a preheated oven at 450 degrees on the top shelf for ten minutes. Take it out from the oven and let it cool.

SERVING SIZE: one
TOTAL SERVINGS: forty

AMOUNT PER SERVING:
Calories	270.00 kcal
Total fat	10.00 g
Cholesterol	0.00 mg
Sodium	95.00 mg
Total carbohydrate	44.00 g
Dietary fiber	3.00 g
Protein	3.00 g

NOTE:
You will find the maamool wooden mold at any Middle Eastern grocery store. Dates have high tannin content and are used medicinally as detersive (having cleansing power) and astringent for intestinal trouble. Dates may be administered for a sore throat or bronchitis.

PASTRY DOUGH STUFFED WITH PISTACHIOS (maamool bil fustok)

INGREDIENTS:

Stuffing: 1 lb. and 6 oz. crushed pistachios, ½ cup sugar, 1/8 cup rosewater,

Dough: 3 lb. and 5 oz. farina, 1½ cup flour, ½ cup sugar, ½ tsp. mahlab (black cherry kernel), 2 ¼ cups I Can't Believe It's Not Butter!®, ¼ cup orange blossom water, ¼ cup lukewarm water, one packet yeast,1/4 tsp. sugar powdered sugar to garnish, wooden mold shaper

BAKING:

Mix the yeast with ¼ cup lukewarm water; sprinkle with ¼ tsp. sugar and set aside to rise.

Mix the pistachios, ½ cup sugar and the rosewater and set aside. Place farina, flour, ½ cup sugar, and mahlab in a bowl and mix well. Add to the mixture the melted butter and rub the mixture with your hand to blend the butter with all the mixture. Add the orange blossom water and the yeast and mix lightly with your fingers; don't knead. Cover and set aside for about five hours. Take a piece of the dough the size of a walnut, place it in your left hand palm and with your right hand index finger make a deep dent in the dough and press against your palm to make the dough like a cup. Fill the cup with some stuffing and gently close the dough over the stuffing; then place it in the wooden mold and press in gently to make the bottom of the maamool flat. Turn the mold upside down and hit it at the edge of the table to release it and drop on your palm. Place all the maamool on a greased baking sheet and set aside for one hour. Bake in a preheated 450 degree oven on the top shelf for ten minutes; take it out from the oven and sprinkle with the powdered sugar and let it cool.

SERVING SIZE: one
TOTAL SERVINGS: thirty

AMOUNT PER SERVING:

Calories	210.00 kcal
Total fat	114.00 g
Cholesterol	0.00 mg
Sodium	40.00 mg
Total carbohydrate	18.00 g
Dietary fiber	2.00 g
Protein	5.00 g

NOTE:

Wooden molds are sold at any Middle Eastern grocery store. Pistachios are high in niacin, Vitamin B$_6$, and manganese, also contains Vitamin C, calcium, iron, magnesium, phosphorus, potassium and zinc. (You can substitute the butter with rendered butter).

PASTRY DOUGH STUFFED WITH WALNUTS (maamool bil joz)

INGREDIENTS:
Stuffing: 1 lb. and 6 oz. crushed walnuts, ½ cup sugar, 1/8 cup rosewater,
Dough: 3 lb. and 5 oz. farina, 1½ cup flour, ½ cup sugar, ½ tsp. mahlab (black cherry kernel),
2 ¼ cups I Can't Believe It's Not Butter!®, ¼ cup orange blossom water, ¼ cup lukewarm water, one yeast packet, ¼ tsp. sugar, powdered sugar to garnish, wooden mold shaper

BAKING:
Mix the yeast with ¼ cup lukewarm water; sprinkle with ¼ tsp. sugar and set aside to rise.
Mix the walnuts, ½ cup sugar and the rosewater and set aside. Place farina, flour, ½ cup sugar, and mahlab in a bowl and mix well. Add to the mixture the melted butter and rub the mixture with your hand to blend the butter with all the mixture. Add the orange blossom water and the yeast and mix lightly with your fingers; don't knead. Cover and set aside for about five hours. Take a piece of the dough the size of a walnut, place it in your left hand palm and with your right hand index finger make a deep dent in the dough and press against your palm to make the dough like a cup. Fill the cup with some stuffing and gently close the dough over the stuffing; then place it in the wooden mold and press in gently to make the bottom of the maamool flat. Turn the mold upside down and hit it at the edge of the table to release it and drop on your palm. Place all the maamool on a greased baking sheet and set aside for one hour. Bake in a preheated 450 degree oven on the top shelf for ten minutes; take it out from the oven and sprinkle with the powdered sugar and let it cool.

SERVING SIZE: one
TOTAL SERVINGS: thirty

_____

AMOUNT PER SERVING:

Calories	210.00 kcal
Total fat	8.00 g
Cholesterol	20.00 mg
Sodium	50.00 mg
Total carbohydrate	29.00 g
Dietary fiber	2.00 g
Protein	2.00 g

NOTE:
Wooden molds are sold at any Middle Eastern grocery store. On October 11, 2006, Science Daily published a report which stated "New research shows that consuming a handful of raw walnuts along with meals high in saturated fat appears to limit the ability of the harmful fat to damage arteries."

SESAME SEED COOKIES (barazek)

INGREDIENTS:

1 cup rendered butter, ½ cup eggbeaters or two eggs
1 cup sugar, 3 cups flour, ¼ cup milk
1 tsp. baking powder
1/2 cups toasted sesame seeds
1/8 cup heavy sugar syrup (attir) or honey
1/8 cup chopped pistachios, ¼ tsp. salt

PREPARING AND BAKING:

Cream the butter, eggs and the sugar and set aside.
Mix the baking powder, salt and the flour very well and add to the egg mixture. Add the milk and knead to form a bread dough consistency. Take a piece of the dough the size of a walnut (1/8 cup) and roll it between your palms to form balls. On a greased baking sheet, place 12 pinches of the crushed pistachio nuts and space them equally. On another flat tray, spread the sesame seeds all over the tray; shake the tray for the sesame seeds to settle flat. Take one dough ball; press it between your palms to flatten it to about 2 ½ inches. Brush the one surface of the flattened dough with some attir or honey and lay that side down on the sesame seeds. Pick up the cookie from the sesame seeds and lay the other side of the cookie down on the pistachio pinches; (the sesame seeds side up). Bake in a preheated oven at 350 degrees for 20 minutes.

SERVING SIZE: one cookie
TOTAL SERVINGS: thirty three

AMOUNT PER SERVING:

Calories	126.47 kcal
Total fat	8.81 g
Cholesterol	15.06 mg
Sodium	5.61 mg
Total carbohydrate	14.85 g
Dietary fiber	0.67 g
Protein	1.18 g

NOTE:

To make heavy sugar syrup (attir), see the sugar syrup recipe in this chapter and change the ratio to two cups sugar and half cup water.

SPICED BISCUITS (bascaut bil bharat)

INGREDIENTS:

2 lbs. flour, 1 tsp. ground cinnamon, ½ tsp. ground clove (powder)
1 tsp. ground nutmeg, 2 tbsp. mahlab, 1 tsp. allspice
½ tsp. baking powder, ½ tsp. baking soda
2 egg whites, 1 ½ cups sugar
1 cup I Can't Believe It's Not Butter!®
½ cup olive oil, 1 cup cheese milk or skim milk
2 yeast packets, 1/2 cup lukewarm water, ¼ tsp. sugar

BAKING:

Mix the yeast with the lukewarm water, sprinkle with 1/4 tsp. sugar cover and let it rise.

Mix flour, cinnamon, ground clove powder, mahlab, ground nutmeg, allspice, baking powder and baking soda and set aside.

Cream the sugar, butter, oil and egg whites and set aside. Place the flour mixture, the egg mixture, the yeast mixture and the milk into a dough mixer, or in a mixing bowl if you want to mix by hand, and knead well. Cover the dough with a cloth and let set for half an hour. Divide the dough into sixty-two parts the size of a walnut; shape it into an oval shape then press it flat and place on a baking sheet. Then, score the top with the back of a fork to decorate and brush with egg whites. Place the sheet on the lower rack and bake in a preheated oven at 350 degrees for 25 minutes; then place it on the top rack for another six minutes. Enjoy with a cup of coffee, demitasse or tea.

SERVING SIZE: one
TOTAL SERVINGS: sixty two

AMOUNT PER SERVING:

Calories	94.66 kcal
Total fat	4.49 g
Cholesterol	0.00 mg
Sodium	14.65 mg
Total carbohydrate	15.93 g
Dietary fiber	0.43 g
Protein	1.80 g

NOTE:

If you don't make cheese to use cheese milk, use skim milk.

STUFFED FILLO DOUGH WITH RICOTTA (m'tabbak)

INGREDIENTS:
Dough: one pound fillo dough (one box), one cup melted rendered (sweet) butter
Stuffing: 2 lbs. ricotta, ½ cup sugar, 1/8 cup orange blossom water and ½ tsp. cinnamon
Dipping: one cup attir (see recipe in this chapter)

PREPARING:
Mix the stuffing ingredients together and set aside.

Open the fillo dough box and lay the sheets flat on the counter. Cover the fillo dough with a damp linen cloth; this is to keep the fillo from drying. Take one sheet of the fillo dough (the size is 16"x12); brush the dough lightly with the melted butter and fold in half. Now you have reduced the size to an 8"x12"sheet; brush the sheet with the butter. Take one heaping tsp. of the stuffing mixture and place in the very top center of the 8" length. Fold one third of the 8" length over the mixture and brush with butter, and then fold the other one third over and brush with butter. Now fold over about 3" where the mixture is at and fold again in the same direction until you have about a 2 3/4"x3" m'tabbak. Lay the finished m'tabbak on a greased baking tray and brush each of them with butter until you finish all the butter. Bake in a preheated oven at 350 degrees for forty-five minutes. Remove from the oven and dip each one in the attir and place them on a serving plate.

SERVING SIZE: one
TOTAL SERVINGS: twenty eight

AMOUNT PER SERVING:

Calorie	170.11 kcal
Total fat	10.03 g
Cholesterol	17.14 mg
Sodium	155.61 mg
Total carbohydrate	21.07 g
Dietary fiber	0.35 g
Protein	3.68 g

NOTE:
When you brush the fillo sheets with the butter, brush them lightly.

Enjoy the m'tabbak at room temperature as a dessert or have it for breakfast.

You can shape the m'tabbak to any shape you wish: you can make them squares, triangle, rectangular, small or large; use your judgment.

STUFFED PANCAKES (atayef)

INGREDIENTS:

Pancake dough: 2 cups flour, 2 ½ cups water, and dash of salt, 2 tbsp. dry yeast, ½ cup lukewarm water, ½ tsp. sugar
Stuffing: 2 cups finely crushed walnuts, ½ cup sugar, 1 tsp. ground cinnamon, 1/8 cup orange blossom water (maazahir). Oil for frying, sugar syrup (attir) for dipping

COOKING:

Dissolve the yeast with 1/2 cup lukewarm water, sprinkle with the sugar cover and set aside to rise. Place the flour, 2 1/2 cups of water, salt and yeast in a dough mixing machine and knead on low speed then increase it gradually to high speed and knead for one minute. Place the dough in a bowl, cover and set aside to rise for about forty minutes. Stir the dough every fifteen minutes to prevent it from separating. Mix the walnuts, sugar, cinnamon and mazahir together and set aside. Heat a pancake griddle well then drop a heaping ¼ cup of the dough on the griddle to make about three inch in diameter pancake. Remove from the griddle when pores form on the surface of the pancake; place the pancake on a large tray one next to another to cool. Place one pancake on your left hand and pinch one end of the pancake to start folding it. Place one heaping tablespoon of the stuffing in the middle of the pancake then continue pinching the edges together to seal and form a half-moon shape atayef. (See the picture). Deep fry the atayef in hot oil until golden brown. Take the atayef out of the hot oil and place on towel paper to drain the oil; place the atayef in the sugar syrup (the attir); then remove from the atir and place on a serving platter. Enjoy as a dessert or as a breakfast treat.

SERVING SIZE: one atayef
TOTAL SERVINGS: sixteen

AMOUNT PER SERVING:

Calories	221.86 kcal
Total fat	1 4.28 g
Cholesterol	0.00 mg
Sodium	1.06 mg
Total carbohydrate	20.10 g
Dietary fiber	1.07 g
Protein	3.23 g

NOTE:

Also you can stuff the pancake with ricotta using the same method. This sweet is traditionally served on St. Barbara's day in September, but of course you can enjoy this dessert any time.

SUGAR COOKIES (ghraybeh)

INGREDIENTS:
2 cups flour
½ cup powdered sugar
2 cups I Can't Believe It's Not Butter!®
35 pistachio nuts
1 tbsp. vanilla extract

BAKING:
Mix all the ingredients together to create the dough and set aside for ten minutes.
Take a piece about 1/8 of a cup from the dough.
Roll the dough between your palms to form a snake shape.
Fold the dough over to join the ends and make it the shape of a donut.
Place the donuts on a baking sheet and press one pistachio over the folded part.
Bake in a preheated oven at 400 degrees for fifteen minutes.
Remove from the oven and set aside to cool very well.
Store the ghraybeh in a cool place.

SERVING SIZE: one
TOTAL SERVING: thirty five

AMOUNT PER SERVING:

Calories	115.94 kcal
Total fat	0.85 g
Cholesterol	0.00 mg
Sodium	0.02 mg
Total carbohydrate	7.88 g
Dietary fiber	0.22 g
Protein	0.17 g

NOTE:
Serve with a cup of Arabic coffee or cup of tea.

SUGAR SYRUP (attir)

INGREDIENTS:

2 cups sugar
1 cup of water
1 tbsp. lemon juice
1 tsp. mazahir (orange blossom water)

COOKING:

Place sugar and water in a sauce pan and bring to a boil.
Add the lemon juice and boil for another ten minutes.
Let it cool, and then add the mazahir.

SERVING SIZE: one tbsp. atir
TOTAL SERVINGS: thirty six

AMOUNT PER SERVING:

Calories	43.00 kcal
Total fat	0.00 g
Cholesterol	0.00 mg
Sodium	0.10 mg
Total carbohydrate	11.10 g
Dietary fiber	0.00 g
Protein	0.00 g

NOTE:

Sugar syrup (attir) is a major recipe used with most Arabic sweets.
Also, you can make attir with Splenda (sugar free).

TURMERIC TEA CAKE (s'foof)

INGREDIENTS:
3 cups fine farina (smeed), 1 cup flour
3 tbs. turmeric, 2 cups milk
1 cup Mazola oil
2 cups sugar
3 tsp. baking powder
Tahineh to grease the tray

PREPARING AND BAKING:
Mix the flour, farina, sugar, turmeric and baking powder very well. Add the oil and the milk and mix again. Grease a baking tray 12" in diameter with one or two tbsp. of tahineh (sesame seed paste).
Pour the mixture in the tray and level it off. Bake in a preheated oven at 350 degrees for forty minutes.
Take the tray out of the oven and set aside to cool.
Cut the s'foof to the shape you like.

SERVING SIZE: one piece
TOTAL SERVINGS: twenty four

AMOUNT PER SERVING:
Calories	221.95 kcal
Total fat	9.89 g
Cholesterol	1.60 mg
Sodium	161.87 mg
Total carbohydrate	31.67 g
Dietary fiber	0.57 g
Protein	2.32 g

NOTE:
Usually the s'foof is cut into diamond shapes.
Serve with a cup of tea.
Turmeric is currently being investigated for possible benefits in Alzheimer's disease, cancer, arthritis, and other clinical disorders.
Turmeric is mostly used in savory dishes as well as some sweet dishes, such as the s'foof cake.

PICKLING

CRUSHED GREEN OLIVES (zaitoon m'faash)

INGREDIENTS:
2 qtrs. raw small fresh green olives *
½ cup pickling salt
5 cups water
Hot pepper optional
1/8 cup olive oil

PICKLING:
First wash the olives thoroughly.

On a hard surface and with a hard object crack the olives without damaging the pit.

Place the cracked olives in a container and cover with water and set aside for six to eight days or until bitterness of the olives disappears.

Place sliced lemon against the inside wall of a jar then add the olives to the middle of the jar.

Mix the salt with the five cups of water and add to the jar, also add the hot pepper if you want the olives to be spicy.

Add the olive oil to prevent the air to go into the jar and spoil the olives.

Store the jar in a cool place or refrigerate. The olives will be ready in a week to consume.

SERVING SIZE: six olives
TOTAL SERVINGS: see below

AMOUNT PER SERVING:
Calories	20.00 kcal
Total fat	1.00 g
Cholesterol	0.00 mg
Sodium	600.00 mg
Total carbohydrate	2.00 g
Dietary fiber	2.00 g
Protein	0.00 g

NOTE:
*Use firm, raw, small green olives.

You can use the same method for curing large green olives.

Also, using this method with large Greek olives, instead of crushing them, slit each one with a knife before soaking in water.

PICKLING CUCUMBER (khiar)

INGREDIENTS:
5 lbs. Kirby cucumbers or 5 lbs. Armenian cucumbers
3 ½ tbsp. pickling salt, 3 ½ cups white vinegar, 3 ½ cups water, 1 tbsp. sugar
5 cloves garlic, 1/4 tsp. red hot pepper flakes
1 tbsp. dry coriander seeds, ¼ cup pickling lime powder

PICKLING:
Dissolve the pickling lime in half gallon water.
Soak the cucumbers in the pickling lime water overnight.
Rinse the cucumbers very well.
In a clean glass jar place garlic, red hot pepper and dry coriander.
Place the cucumbers in the jar.
In a cooking pot dissolve the pickling salt with the water, add the white vinegar and bring mixture to a boil.
Pour the boiling water into the jar. Sprinkle the sugar on the top.
Cover the jar tightly with the lid.
Flip the jar upside down for two days then flip it back to upright.
The cucumbers should be ready to eat in about five days.
We recommend refrigerating the jar.

SERVING SIZE: one pickle
TOTAL SERVINGS: eighty

AMOUNT PER SERVING:
Calories	12.00 kcal
Total fat	0.12 g
Cholesterol	0.00 mg
Sodium	833.00 mg
Total carbohydrate	2.68 g
Dietary fiber	0.80 g
Protein	0.40 g

NOTE:
With the same method you can pickle cauliflower also.
Evidence indicates that the cucumber has been cultivated in western Asia and listed among the foods of the ancient times of Greece and the Middle East.

PICKLING EGGPLANTS (baitinjan makbous)

INGREDIENTS:

10 small eggplants about one and half pounds
10 small cloves garlic or five large cloves (mashed)
¼ cup chopped fresh red pepper
¼ cup chopped fine celery
Pinch of hot pepper flakes,
3 ½ cups water, 3 ½ tbsp. pickling salt
3 ½ cups white vinegar, 1 tbsp. sugar

PREPARING:

Mix celery, garlic, red pepper and hot pepper flakes and set aside.
Dissolve the salt with the water add the white vinegar and bring to a boil; then set aside to cool. Place the eggplants in a pot and cover with water.
Place a plate on the top of the eggplants and place a weight on the top of this plate to prevent the eggplants from floating to the top of the pot.
Bring to a boil, and cook for half an hour.
Drain the water and set aside the eggplants to cool.
Slit the side of each eggplant and stuff with some of the celery mixture.
Place the eggplants in a clean glass jar, and then add the cooled pickling water mixture.
Add the sugar and cover with the lid: keep outside for five days before you refrigerate.

SERVING SIZE: one eggplant
TOTAL SERVINGS: twenty

AMOUNT PER SERVING:

Calories	32.50 kcal
Total fat	1.96 g
Cholesterol	0.00 mg
Sodium	129.24 mg
Total carbohydrate	8.24 g
Dietary fiber	2.85 g
Protein	1.14 g

NOTE:

The eggplant pickles are delicious next to m'jadara and other meals.

PICKLING TURNIPS (liffit)

INGREDIENTS:
5 lbs. turnips, 3 ½ tbsp. pickling salt
3 ½ cups white vinegar, 3 ½ cups cold water
5 cloves garlic minced, ½ tsp. red pepper flakes
1 small beet boiled, skinned and cut into four pieces
1 tsp. sugar

PICKLING:
Wash the turnips thoroughly and cut out the damaged and the hard spots.
Cut each to four pieces or to six pieces if the turnips are large.
Stack them in a one gallon glass jar.
Add the rest of the ingredients to the jar and close the lid tightly.
Flip the jar upside down and set aside for two days, and then flip it upright.
The turnips should be ready to eat in about five days then refrigerate.

SERVING SIZE: 3.5 ounce
TOTAL SERVINGS: twenty three

AMOUNT PER SERVING:

Calories	27.00 kcal
Total fat	0.10 g
Cholesterol	0.00 mg
Sodium	67.00 mg
Total carbohydrate	6.23 g
Dietary fiber	1.80 g
Protein	0.90 g

NOTE:
Turnips are popular in most countries and used in different recipes but, in the Middle Eastern countries, turnips are pickled.
Turnips (greens) are a good source of Vitamin A, folate, Vitamin C, Vitamin K and calcium.

SLIT BLACK OR KALAMATA OLIVES (zaitoon m'jarrah)

INGREDIENTS:
2 quarts raw small black olives or Kalamata*
½ cup pickling salt
5 cups water
1/8 cup olive oil

PICKLING:
First wash the olives thoroughly.
With a knife, slit the side of every olive.
Place the olives in a container and cover with water and set aside for six to eight days or until the olives are no longer bitter, change the water twice a day.
Place slices of lemon against the inside wall of the jar then add the olives to the glass jar.
Mix the salt and water and add to the jar.
Add the olive oil to prevent the air to go into the jar and spoil the olives.

SERVING SIZE: six olives
TOTAL SERVINGS: see below

_____

AMOUNT PER SERVING:

Calories	20.00 kcal
Total fat	1.00 g
Cholesterol	0.00 mg
Sodium	600.00 mg
Total carbohydrate	2.00 g
Dietary fiber	2.00 g
Protein	0.00 g

NOTE:
*Fresh, firm olives.
You can use the same method for curing large green olives.
Also use the same method with large Greek olives.

STUFFED EGGPLANT WITH WALNUTS (makdoos)

INGREDIENTS:
10 medium size eggplants (about two pounds), 10 mashed garlic cloves in one tsp. salt
½ cup finely crushed walnuts, one cup olive oil

PICKLING:
Place the eggplants in a four quart pot, place a plate and weight on the top of the eggplant to prevent them from floating to the top, add water to the pot to cover the eggplants and bring it to a boil; then reduce the heat to medium and boil the eggplants for 25 minutes or until you can easily remove the eggplant crowns. Remove the pot place it under running cold water to stop the process of cooking. When the eggplants cool, slit the side of each one, then wet your right thumb with water and dip it in salt. Hold one eggplant with your left hand, the neck of the eggplant up. Stick your right thumb in the eggplant and rub the salt in. Move your thumb toward the neck of the eggplant and with your left hand gently squeeze around the thumb and you will see the liquid coming out of the eggplant. Move your thumb to the bottom of the eggplant and again squeeze any remaining liquid. After you squeeze the liquid out of all the eggplants, place them in a colander the slit side down and cover with towel paper and then a plate and a weight on the top. Set aside to drain the remaining liquid. On the next day, mix the walnuts and the garlic together and evenly stuff the mixture in each eggplant. Now line up the stuffed eggplants in a clean glass jar the slit side up. Stuff some towel paper in the jar, cover the jar with the lid and flip it upside down and set aside for at least eight hours to drain more liquid. Set the jar right side up, take the towel papers out and add olive oil to cover the eggplants. Cover the jar and set aside in a cool place for three days. Now the makdoos is ready to be consumed. Refrigerate the makdoos to last for some time. Stuff one makdoos in pita bread and enjoy as a sandwich.

SERVING SIZE: one
TOTAL SERVINGS: ten

AMOUNT PER SERVING:

Calories	155.65 kcal
Total fat	13.40 g
Cholesterol	0.00 mg
Sodium	27.22 mg
Total carbohydrate	8.70 g
Dietary fiber	3.23 g
Protein	2.76 g

STUFFED GREEN BELL PEPPERS (flaifleh mihshieh)

INGREDIENTS:

6 large green peppers (remove the crown, wash and discard seeds)
1 cup carrots (chopped),
1 cup string beans (chopped)
1 cup boiled cabbage (chopped)
1 cup celery (chopped),
1 cup cauliflower (florets separated)
4 cups diced cucumber
3 ½ cups water
3 ½ cups white vinegar, 3 ½ tbsp. salt, 1 tbsp. sugar
1 tsp. hot pepper flakes (optional)

PREPARING AND PICKLING:

Mix carrots, string beans, cucumber, cabbage, celery and cauliflower.
Rinse the pepper and stuff with the carrot mixture and place in a large glass jar or plastic container. Boil water, vinegar and salt and pour to the bell pepper; the vinegar mixture should cover the pepper. Add the hot pepper flakes and the sugar. Close the jar and leave it at room temperature until the bell peppers change color and taste like a pickle. Keep in a cool place or refrigerate.

SERVING SIZE: quarter of pepper
TOTAL SERVINGS: twenty four

AMOUNT PER SERVING:

Calories	15.93 kcal
Total fat	0.12 g
Cholesterol	0.00 mg
Sodium	110.00 mg
Total carbohydrate	4.23 g
Dietary fiber	1.36 g
Protein	0.70 g

NOTE:

Stuff half of pita bread with the pickle mixture and enjoy as a snack.
Also, you can pickle the green peppers cut into strips, without stuffing.

PUDDINGS AND ICE CREAM

HOMEMADE CREAM (ishta)

INGREDIENTS:

3 cups powdered milk
¼ cup all-purpose flour
4 cups water

MAKING:

Mix the milk powder and the flour together very well.
Place the mixture in a pot and dissolve it with the water.
Bring to a boil, reduce the heat and cook until the mixture thickens.
Stir constantly to prevent the mixture from sticking to the bottom of the pot and burn.
Pour the mixture in a large tray and set aside to cool.
Remove the ishta from the tray and place it in a container.
Refrigerate the container for future use.

SERVING SIZE: quarter of a cup
TOTAL SERVINGS: thirty

AMOUNT PER SERVING:

Calories	22.08 kcal
Total fat	0.00 g
Cholesterol	1.25 mg
Sodium	31.25 mg
Total carbohydrate	4.45 g
Dietary fiber	0.02 g
Protein	2.01 g

NOTE:

You can use the cream instead of ricotta in the sweets chapter.
Also, you can add it as a topping to the Syrian ice cream.

PUDDING TRAY (aish el saraya)

INGREDIENTS:

6 cups soy milk (vanilla)
1 cup sugar (Splenda)
3/4 cup corn starch
2 cups attir (syrup)
8 slices of white bread (edges trimmed)
1/4 cups crushed raw pistachio nuts.

COOKING:

In a 9''x15'' Pyrex tray lay down the slices of bread tight one next to the other.
Bake in a preheated oven at 350 degrees until the top of the bread is light brown.
Take the tray out and pour the syrup over the bread and set aside.
Dissolve the cornstarch in half a cup of the cold soy milk.
Place the rest of the soy milk, sugar and the dissolved starch in a cooking pot.
Cook on medium heat stirring constantly till the mixture thickens.
Pour the mixture in the tray over the bread and level it off by shaking the tray.
Garnish with the pistachios and let it cool.
Cut with a knife to 15 squares and serve.

SERVING SIZE: one square
TOTAL SERVING: fifteen

AMOUNT PER SERVING:

Calories	198.8 0 kcal
Total fat	2.60 g
Cholesterol	0.00 mg
Sodium	86.00 mg
Total carbohydrate	42.20 g
Dietary fiber	0.80 g
Protein	3.90 g

NOTE:

You can add more syrup if desired.
You have the option to use regular milk, 2% reduced milk or half and half; also you can use granular sugar instead of Splenda.

RICE PUDDING (riz b'haleeb)

INGREDIENTS:
4 cups low fat milk, ½ cup long grain rice
1 tbsp. corn starch dissolved in ¼ cup water
1 cup sugar, ¼ cup egg white
3 tbsp. orange blossom water, 1 tsp. cinnamon (optional)
½ tsp. vanilla extract, 1/4 tsp. ground fine Arabic gum dissolved with 1 tsp. water
¼ c crushed pistachio nuts

COOKING:
Place the milk in a cooking pot then add the rice without rinsing.
Place the pot in the refrigerator overnight or for at least 5 hours.
Place the pot on high heat and bring to a boil stirring all the time.
Reduce the heat to low, cover the pot and cook for 30 minutes or until the rice becomes tender.
Add the sugar to the pot and stir for about three minutes for the sugar to dissolve.
Dissolve the corn starch with the water and add to it the egg white, Arabic gum, the vanilla extract; mix and add to the pot and stir the mixture until it thickens. Stir in the orange blossom water, then pour into a serving plate or individual small plates and garnish with the cinnamon and pistachio nuts.

SERVING SIZE: half cup
TOTAL SERVINGS: twelve

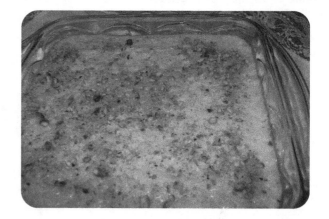

AMOUNT PER SERVING:
Calories	125.15 kcal
Total fat	4.31 g
Cholesterol	6.67 mg
Sodium	31.88 mg
Total carbohydrate	25.46 g
Dietary fiber	0.29 g
Protein	4.14 g

NOTE:
The cinnamon and the pistachio nuts are optional.
You can garnish the rice pudding with your favorite nuts.

SYRIAN ICE CREAM (booza)

INGREDIENTS:
½ gallon whole milk
1 pint heavy cream
2 ½ cups sugar
3 tsp. sahlab
½ tsp. powdered Arabic gum (miskeh)
Ice cream salt

PREPARATION:
In a large pot, mix the milk and the heavy cream and heat to lukewarm.
Add sugar, Arabic gum and sahlab and bring to a boil; stir constantly until the mixture thickens.
Remove from the heat and let it cool.

CHURNING:
Place ice cubes in the ice cream bucket with the salt between layers.
Pour the mixture into the inside bucket and churn for about eight minutes then
Place the ice cream in a container and freeze.

SERVING SIZE: one cup
TOTAL SERVINGS: sixteen

_____

AMOUNT PER SERVING:

Calories	238.62 kcal
Total fat	9.72 g
Cholesterol	37.62 mg
Sodium	9.37 mg
Total carbohydrate	35.36 g
Dietary fiber	0.00 g
Protein	4.08 g

NOTE:
Sahlab and miskeh can be purchase at Middle Eastern grocery stores.

SALADS

AND

SPREADS

GARDEN SALAD (salata arabee)

INGREDIENTS:

1 fresh tomato, (about ½ lb.) washed and cut into small pieces
2 cucumbers (about ½ lb.) peeled and cut into small pieces
¼ cup chopped fresh mint leaves or 1 tsp. dry crumbled mint leaves
1 small size chopped sweet onion
½ cup washed and chopped parsley
1 small chopped green or red pepper
1/8 cup olive oil
½ tsp. salt, 1/8 cup lemon juice
¼ tsp. black pepper

TOSSING:

In a salad bowl, combine all the ingredients and toss.

SERVING SIZE: half cup
TOTAL SERVINGS: ten

AMOUNT PER SERVING:

Calories	35.40 kcal
Total fat	2.88 g
Cholesterol	0.00 mg
Sodium	118.83 mg
Total carbohydrate	2.86 g
Dietary fiber	1.53 g
Protein	5.31 g

NOTE:

Here are some of the benefits of eating Arabic garden salad:
The tomatoes in the salad are helpful in preventing prostate cancer. Also, they are an antioxidant and they are high in Vitamin C. The cucumber is crunchy and has a cool taste.
The parsley refreshes bad breath and also is proven to be a kidney stimulant.
The onion has an effect against the common cold and helps diabetes; also is an anti-inflammatory, anti-cholesterol, anti-cancer and antioxidant.
The olive oil (the proportion of monounsaturated fats in the diet) reduces the risk of heart disease.

BBQ EGGPLANT SALAD (baba ghannouj)

INGREDIENTS:
1 eggplant (about 1 lb.), 1 small cut up onion (about 4 oz.)
1 green pepper, about 4 oz., diced and inside seeds removed
1 cup chopped parsley, ¼ cup olive oil
1 fresh tomato (about ½ lb.) diced,
½ tsp. allspice, 3 cloves garlic (mashed with ¾ tsp. salt)
1/8 cup wine vinegar, ¼ tsp. liquid smoke (optional)

MIXING:
Wash the eggplant, and place it on a high flame to scorch the skin by holding the eggplant with a tong and carefully turning it around on the flame to scorch all the skin and to get the inside cooked.
Let the eggplant cool then remove only the burnt skin and discard.
Place cooked eggplant in a salad bowl and mash roughly with a fork. Add remaining ingredients and toss.
Place the eggplant salad in a serving plate and serve at room temperature.
If you do not have a gas stovetop, you can do the process on a barbecue grill or under the broiler.

SERVING SIZE: half cup
TOTAL SERVINGS: ten

AMOUNT PER SERVING:

Calories	72.33 kcal
Total fat	5.63 g
Cholesterol	0.00 mg
Sodium	180.00 mg
Total carbohydrate	6.15 g
Dietary fiber	1.77 g
Protein	0.88 g

NOTE:
The eggplant originated in India. The Arabic name for eggplant is "baitinjan". Eggplant was introduced throughout the Mediterranean Area by the Arabs in the early middle Ages. Studies of the Institute of Sao Paulo State University, Brazil, have shown that eggplant is effective in the treatment of high blood cholesterol but cannot replace statin drugs. In the Arab world, eggplant is used in many dishes as you see in different chapters of this book.

BBQ EGGPLANT DIP (m'tabbal)

INGREDIENTS:
1 large eggplant
1/4 cup tahineh paste
¼ cup low fat plain yogurt
2 mashed garlic cloves
½ tsp. salt
¼ tsp. liquid smoke (optional)

COOKING:
Wash the eggplant, and place it on a high flame to scorch the skin by holding the eggplant with a tong and carefully turning it around on the flame to scorch all the skin and to get the inside softened.
Let the eggplant cool then remove only the burnt skin and discard.
Place cooked eggplant in a salad bowl and mash roughly with a fork.
Add the rest of the ingredients and mix.
Place the mixture in a serving dish and garnish with olive oil and a few pieces of parsley.

SERVING SIZE: ¼ cup
TOTAL SERVINGS: eight

AMOUNT PER SERVING:

Calories	54.20 kcal
Total fat	36.10 g
Cholesterol	3.70 mg
Sodium	162.70 mg
Total carbohydrate	2.50 g
Dietary fiber	1.60 g
Protein	2.00 g

NOTE:
This recipe was carefully put together and was adjusted several times. However, you can adjust it to fit your taste (more or less of the ingredients). It is delicious with pita bread.
For the eggplant origin and health benefit, refer to the baba ghannouj recipe.

BEET SALAD (salatet shawander)

INGREDIENTS:
2 cans sliced beets (14.5 oz. each) or boiled fresh beets
½ cup slivered sweet onion
1/8 cup olive oil, ¼ cup wine vinegar
½ tsp. salt

PREPORATION:
Drain the beets from the canned liquid.
Rinse the beets with cold water.
Place in a salad bowl.
Add the rest of the ingredients and toss.

SERVING SIZE: half cup
TOTAL SERVINGS: eight

AMOUNT PER SERVING:

Calories	63.30 kcal
Total fat	3.30 g
Cholesterol	0.00 mg
Sodium	399.75 mg
Total carbohydrate	8.25 g
Dietary fiber	1.90 g
Protein	0.99 g

NOTE:
How to boil fresh beets:
Remove stems from fresh beets and discard then place fresh beets in a large pot. Cover the beets with water to 1" above the top of the beets. Boil until you can push a fork in the beets and it is removed easily. Peel the skin with your hand while the beets are warm.
It was suggested that by the first century B.C. the domestic beet was presented in the Mediterranean Basin. Now you can find beets everywhere.
Beets move the blood in your veins; help fight cancer and dementia and aid in losing weight.
Beets contain Vitamins A, B and C, thiamine, riboflavin, niacin, folate, calcium, Iron, magnesium, phosphorus, potassium, and zinc.

CABBAGE SALAD (salatet yakhana)

INGREDIENTS:

1 pound shredded cabbage
½ pound sliced tomato
½ cup shredded onion
2 cloves garlic (mashed with 1 tsp. salt)
1 tbsp. crushed mint leaves
¼ cup olive oil
¼ cup apple cider vinegar

TOSS:

In a salad bowl, mix all the ingredients together and toss.
Serve solo or next to the "m'jadara meal".

SERVING SIZE: one cup
TOTAL SERRVINGS: eight

AMOUNT PER SERVING:

Calories	109.72 kcal
Total fat	6.98 g
Cholesterol	0.00 mg
Sodium	313.03 mg
Total carbohydrate	5.64 g
Dietary fiber	1 .78 g
Protein	3.17 g

NOTE:

Cabbage is an excellent source of Vitamin C; it also contains significant amounts of glutamine, an amino acid that has anti-inflammatory properties.
Cabbage also can be included in dieting programs, as it is a low calorie food.
Cabbage contains thiamin, riboflavin, niacin, Vitamin C, Vitamin B, calcium, iron, magnesium, phosphorus, potassium, and zinc.
Cabbage is used in other Middle Eastern dishes, like cabbage rolls and others.

CUCUMBER AND YOGURT SALAD (khiar oo laban)

INGREDIENTS:

2 cups plain yogurt
1 cup cubed cucumber (small cubes)
1 tsp. dried and crumbled mint leaves
1 garlic clove mashed with ½ tsp salt.

PREPARATION:

In a salad bowl, mix the entire ingredients together and refrigerate.
You could mix some crushed ice with it.
If you like garlic add more cloves.

SERVING SIZE: ½ cup
TOTAL SERVINGS: six

_____

AMOUNT PER SERVING:

Calories	36.37 kcal
Total fat	1.29 g
Cholesterol	4.32 mg
Sodium	194.69 mg
Total carbohydrate	6.21 g
Dietary fiber	0.87 g
Protein	4.41 g

NOTE:

Cucumber salad is used solo or next to kifta kabob, shish kabob, kibbeh, ijjeh, and other dishes.
The Spaniards (Christopher Columbus) brought the cucumber to Haiti in 1494.
And Jacques Cartier, French explorer, found "very great cucumbers" grown on the site where Montréal is now.
Cucumbers originated in India and have been cultivated for at least 3000 years in western Asia.
For a yogurt explanation, see "Making Yogurt".

FAVA BEAN SALAD (fool m'dammas)

INGREDIENTS:
1 16 oz. can dry cooked fava beans, 1 16 oz. can garbanzo beans
1/2 cup chopped onion, 1 cup chopped fresh tomato
1 cup chopped parsley, 1/3 cup olive oil
3 cloves garlic mashed, 3 tbsp. red wine vinegar
1 tsp. salt, 1/2 tsp. allspice

PREPARATION:
Open the garbanzo and the fava beans cans place them in a strainer and rinse them with hot water. Place the garbanzo and the fava beans in a cooking pot, cover with hot water and bring to a boil.
Cook for ten minutes then drain and place in a salad bowl.
Add the rest of the ingredients and toss.
Enjoy with Arabic bread.

SERVING SIZE: half cup
TOTAL SERVINGS: nine

AMOUNT PER SERVING:

Calories	157.90 kcal
Total fat	9.20 g
Cholesterol	0.00 mg
Sodium	548.10 mg
Total carbohydrate	14.11 g
Dietary Fiber	3.38 g
Protein	5.66 g

NOTE:
Beans have a significant amount of fiber.
One cup of cooked beans provides between nine and ten grams of fiber.
Soluble fiber can lower blood cholesterol.
Beans are also high in protein, complex carbohydrates, folate and iron.
In the Middle East this meal is served for breakfast.
Also in the Middle East when a person donates blood, after the blood is withdrawn, the doctor's advice to the donor is to have a fool m'dammas meal.

FRIED EGGPLANT SPREAD (m'fassagh)

INGREDIENTS:

1 eggplant about one pound
3 mashed garlic cloves
¾ cup plain yogurt
1 tbsp. tahineh (sesame seed paste)
½ tsp. salt

PREPARING AND MAKING:

Peel the eggplant and slice to about ½" thick.
Spread the eggplant on a plate and sprinkle with salt to drain the liquid from them.
Squeeze the liquid out of the eggplant and fry until the eggplants are browned and soft inside.
Place eggplant on towel papers to absorb the oil.
Mash the eggplant with a fork and mix with the rest of the ingredients.
Place in a serving plate and garnish with fresh mint leaves.

SERVING SIZE: quarter of a cup
TOTAL SERVINGS: ten

AMOUNT PER SERVING:

Calories	34.10 kcal
Total fat	34.10 g
Cholesterol	1.12 mg
Sodium	131.88 mg
Total carbohydrate	5.41 g
Dietary fiber	1.30 g
Protein	1.66 g

NOTE:

Serve this plate next to any meal of kibbeh.
Or as a sandwich stuff it in pita bread with couple slices of fresh tomatoes and, slivered sweet onion and few fresh mint leaves or as an appetizer.
For the history and the health benefit of the eggplant see "b.b.q eggplant salad (baba ghannouj)".
For the history and the health benefit of yogurt see "making yogurt (laban)".

HUMMUS (m'sabaha)

INGREDIENTS:
2 cups garbanzo beans (15.5 oz. can) or dried garbanzo home cooked
1/4 cup tahineh (sesame seed paste)
1/4 cup water
1/4 cup lemon juice
1 clove garlic
1/2 tsp. salt

PREPARATION:
Rinse the beans clear of canned liquid; then boil in fresh water for about 15 minutes and drain the water. Place all ingredients in a blender and process until the mixture becomes creamy.
Place the hummus in a plate and garnish with olive oil, chopped parsley, sprinkle of paprika, and black seeds (optional, see picture).

SERVING SIZE IS: ¼ cup
TOTAL SERVINGS: eight

AMOUNT PER SERVING:

Calories	94.00 kcal
Total fat	5.00 g
Cholesterol	0.00 mg
Sodium	324.00 mg
Total carbohydrate	9.00 g
Dietary fiber	2.00 g
Protein	5.00 g

NOTE:
All the ingredients except the (garbanzo) are flexible; you can add or reduce the amount according to your taste.
Garbanzo beans are a helpful source of zinc and protein.
Also they are very high in dietary fiber. Garbanzo beans are a healthy source of carbohydrate for people with insulin and diabetes sensitivity.
And garbanzo beans are low in fat and mostly polyunsaturated.
Garbanzo beans also provide dietary calcium.

KIDNEY AND GARBANZO BEAN SALAD (salatet fasoulieh hamra)

INGREDIENTS:
1 can kidney beans (15.25 oz.), 1 can garbanzo beans (15.5 oz.)
1 cup chopped parsley
1 cup chopped sweet onion
2 mashed garlic cloves, 1 tsp. salt
1/2 tsp. allspice, ¼ cup red wine vinegar
¼ cup olive oil

COOKING:
Open the cans of garbanzo and kidney beans; rinse well with water. Place the beans in a pot, cover with water and bring to a boil.
Reduce the heat to low; cover the pot and cook for 20 to30 minutes or until you feel the beans are soft and tender. Then drain them from the water and place them in a mixing bowl.
Add the parsley, onion, garlic, salt, allspice, vinegar and the olive oil and toss.
Transfer the mixture to a serving plate and serve next to Arabic pita bread at room temperature.

SERVING SIZE: half a cup
TOTAL SERVINGS: eight

AMOUNT PER SERVING:
Calories	167.58 kcal
Total fat	9.44 g
Cholesterol	0.00 mg
Sodium	314.34 mg
Total carbohydrate	15.75g
Dietary fiber	4.16 g
Protein	6.71 g

NOTE:
Stuff this salad in a half pita pocket bread and enjoy as a sandwich. Garbanzo or "hummus" beans were found in Jericho and Turkey in ancient times. They are a helpful source of zinc, folate and protein and are high in dietary fiber. Kidney beans have good health benefits. are a proven kidney stimulant.

MUSHROOM SALAD (salatet fitir)

INGREDIENTS:

20 mushrooms about 8 oz., ½ medium size onion (slivered)
½ cup chopped parsley, ¼ cup olive oil
¼ cup lemon juice
½ tsp. salt, 3 cloves garlic (mashed with the salt)

PREPARATION:

Wash the mushrooms thoroughly.
Then boil until they get tender (about 20 minutes) and drain.
Slice the mushrooms to quarters.
Place the mushrooms in a salad bowl.
Add the rest of the ingredients and toss.

SERVING SIZE: half cup
TOTAL SERVINGS: eight

AMOUNT PER SERVING:

Calories	44.58 kcal
Total fat	3.57 g
Cholesterol	0.00 mg
Sodium	147.91 mg
Total carbohydrate	3.24 g
Dietary fiber	1.08 g
Protein	0.85 g

NOTE:

Mushrooms are popular in many cuisines especially Chinese, European and Japanese.
Many species of mushrooms are high in dietary fiber, also in protein and vitamins such as, thiamin, riboflavin, niacin, biotin, cobalamins, and ascorbic acid.
Mushrooms are a source of some minerals, including, selenium, potassium, and phosphorus.

PARSLEY SALAD (Tabbouleh)

INGREDIENTS:
3 cups finely chopped parsley (2 bunches)
1/2 cup finely chopped sweet onion
2 cups diced fresh tomato
2 tbsp. dry mint leaves or (fresh mint leaves)
1/4 cup number #1 bulgur
1 tbsp. tomato paste, 1 tsp. salt
1/2 tsp. allspice, 1/4 cup olive oil
1/4 cup fresh lemon juice

PREPARATION:
In a large salad bowl, dilute the tomato paste with two tbsp. water and the lemon juice. Then add the bulgur and diced fresh tomato and mix well and let it stand for 30 minutes to soften the bulgur. Add the rest of the ingredients and toss.
Serve with romaine lettuce leaves as an appetizer.

SERVING SIZE: half a cup
TOTAL SERVINGS: ten

AMOUNT PER SERVING:

Calories	73.90 kcal
Total fat	12.90 g
Cholesterol	0.00 mg
Sodium	252.80 mg
Total carbohydrate	5.60 g
Dietary Fiber	1.00 g
Protein	1.30 g

NOTE:
Parsley is an herb and often used as a spice. Also, it is common in Middle Eastern cooking. Chinese and German horologists recommend parsley tea to help control high blood pressure. Cherokee Indians used the parsley as a tonic to strengthen the bladder.
When the parsley is crushed and rubbed on the skin, it is said to reduce itching of mosquito bites. Also, parsley is proven to be a kidney stimulant. Parsley contains thiamine, riboflavin, niacin, Vitamin B, Vitamin C, Vitamin K, calcium, iron, magnesium, phosphorus, potassium, and zinc.

PITA BREAD SALAD (Fattoush)

INGREDIENTS:

½ loaf pita bread (cut to about 1"squares and toasted in the oven)
2 heads romaine lettuce (about 12 oz.) rinsed and chopped
1 fresh tomato (about 8 oz.) washed and chopped
3 cloves of garlic (mashed with 2 tsp. salt)
1/8 cup ground sumac, ½ cup olive oil
About 15 pitted black olives (slivered)
½ lb. cucumber (rinsed, peeled and chopped)
½ cup rinsed and chopped parsley
½ cup chopped sweet onion or scallion
10 oz. radishes (cleaned and slivered)
1 tbsp. dried mint leaves (fine dried mint leaves)
¼ cup apple cider vinegar or lemon juice

MIXING:

Place the toasted bread in a mixing bowl. Sprinkle sumac on bread then add ¼ cup oil, garlic and mix well then set aside for l/2 hr. Mix in the rest of the ingredients, add additional salt if necessary; toss and serve.

SERVING SIZE: one cup
TOTAL SERVINGS: twelve

AMOUNT PER SERVING:

Calories	109.49 kcal
Total fat	14.47 g
Cholesterol	0.00 mg
Sodium	23.90 mg
Total carbohydrate	6.72 g
Dietary fiber	1.33 g
Protein	1.32 g

NOTE:

Fattoush is an Arabic word. The word comes from "fattet" or "fatafeet" which is leftover small pieces of pita bread. Fattoush is considered a traditional dish in Syria, Lebanon and other countries in the Middle East. Because of the fresh, delicious ingredients in the recipe, fattoush is also considered a most healthy and vegetarian dish.

POTATO SALAD (M'tawameh)

INGREDIENTS:
1½ lb. potatoes
1 slivered sweet onion
1 cut up tomato
1 cup chopped parsley
4 mashed garlic gloves with 1 tsp. salt
Juice of one lemon
¼ cup olive oil
1 tsp. allspice

COOKING:
Boil the potatoes for about 30 minutes or until you can stick the potatoes with a fork that pierces easily. Drain from the cooking water.
Run cold water over the potatoes to stop the cooking process.
Peel the potatoes and let them cool in the refrigerator before you dice them into about one inch pieces.
Place the potatoes in a salad bowl; add the rest of the ingredients and toss.

SERVING SIZE: one cup
TOTAL SERVINGS: eight

AMOUNT PER SERVING:

Calories	158.93 kcal
Total fat	7.11 g
Cholesterol	0.00 mg
Sodium	301.95 mg
Total carbohydrate	23.23 g
Dietary fiber	13.59 g
Protein	2.51 g

NOTE:
Potatoes are widely popular in the United States and used in several dishes, hot or cold.
For example: potato salad, French fries, hash brown, baked potatoes, mashed potatoes, and many other dishes. The nutrients in potatoes are Vitamin C, Vitamin B6, thiamin, niacin, folate, iron, magnesium, potassium, copper and fiber. The benefit of the fiber is in the skin.

YOGURT SPREAD (Labaneh)

INGREDIENTS:
Yogurt (not fat free)
1 tsp. salt
1/2 tsp. crushed dried mint leaves
1 tbsp. olive oil

COOKING:
See the recipe for making yogurt or purchase already made yogurt from the store.
Pour the yogurt in a yogurt strainer.
Refrigerate overnight, then drain and discard the liquid.
Place the drained labaneh in a flat plate, add the salt, mix and spread it out into serving dish.
Garnish with the mint leaves first, then the oil.
If you do not have a yogurt strainer, place thin cheesecloth in a colander and place the colander within a deep bowl or in the sink. Place the yogurt onto the cheesecloth and follow the instructions above. The yogurt should drain completely before mixing.

SERVING SIZE: 2 tablespoons
TOTAL SERVINGS: forty

AMOUNT PER SERVING:

Calories	60.00 kcal
Total fat	6.00 g
Cholesterol	25.00 mg
Sodium	15.00 mg
Total carbohydrate	1.00 g
Dietary fiber	0.00 g
Protein	1.00 g

NOTE:

Labaneh is nutritionally rich in protein, calcium, Riboflavin, Vitamin B_6, Vitamin B_{12}.
Also labaneh has nutrition benefits beyond those of milk. (See yogurt)

SOUPS

LENTIL SOUP (Shorabet Addas)

INGREDIENTS:

1 cup lentils
5 cups water
1 cup chopped onion
1 tbsp. flour diluted in ¼ cup water
1/8 cup olive oil
1/8 cup lemon juice
½ tsp. allspice, 1 tsp. salt

COOKING:

Rinse the lentils thoroughly and place in a cooking pot with the onion, water, salt and allspice.
Bring to a boil, then reduce the heat to low, cover and let cook for half an hour.
In the meantime, mix the diluted flour with the oil.
Add the oil mixture to the soup and simmer until the lentils are well done.
Add the lemon juice and remove from the stove.
Serve hot with toasted pita bread.

SERVING SIZE: one cup
TOTAL SERVINGS: eight

AMOUNT PER SERVING:

Calories	79.75 kcal
Total fat	3.41 g
Cholesterol	0.00 mg
Sodium	349.90 mg
Total carbohydrate	8.66 g
Dietary Fiber	2.30 g
Protein	2.60 g

NOTE:

If you need to make it less thick, add more water while it is cooking.
(Option 2) add one cup chopped celery and one cup carrots to the lentils at the beginning.

LENTIL SOUP WITH SWISS CHARD (Rishta)

INGREDIENTS:

1 cup rinsed lentils, 10 cups water, and 1 tsp. allspice
2 cups chopped Swiss chard ribs with some leaves
6 cloves garlic (mashed with 1 tsp. salt)
1 cup fresh chopped cilantro
1 can 15 oz. garbanzo beans (drained and rinsed)
1 large chopped onion
2 tbsp. flour (diluted in ¼ cup water), 1/3 cup olive oil
½ cup small elbow macaroni or orzo, ½ cup lemon juice

COOKING:

In a soup cooking pot, combine water, lentils, allspice, garbanzo beans, elbow macaroni, Swiss chard and onion. Bring the mixture to a boil, and then reduce the heat to low, cover the pot and simmer for one-half an hour or until the lentils and the Swiss chard are cooked well. Add the cilantro and garlic to the pot. Add the oil to the diluted flour mix and stir into the Rishta. Cover the pot and cook for another 10 minutes. Add the lemon juice. Remove from the stove and set aside for five minutes. Serve hot with toasted pita bread chips.

SERVING SIZE: one cup
TOTAL SERVINGS: fifteen

AMOUNT PER SERVING:

Calories	121.00 kcal
Total fat	5.30 g
Cholesterol	0.00 mg
Sodium	192.80 mg
Total carbohydrate	14.50 g
Dietary fiber	12.00 g
Protein	7.20 g

NOTE:

There are different kinds of lentils: brown, red, and green. The brown is used in this recipe, "Rishta".
Lentils contain high levels of protein, including the essential amino acids isoleucine and lysine.
Also lentils are one of the best vegetable sources of iron.

PUMPKIN SOUP (Shorabet yaateen)

INGREDIENTS:
1 lb. pumpkin peeled and cubed, 1 lb. potatoes peeled and cubed
4 cans chicken broth about (8 cups), 2 cups water
2 cups chopped onion, 1/2 cup I Can't Believe It's Not Butter!®
1 tsp. cinnamon, 1 cup peeled and chopped tomato
1 tsp. salt, 1 tsp. black pepper

COOKING:
Sauté pumpkin, potatoes and onion with the butter for about 15 minutes
Add the rest of the ingredients and cook for another 15 minutes.
Remove the mixture from the pot and leave only the liquid in the pot.
Puree` the mixture in a blender, then return the puree` to the pot and cook for another 5 minutes
Garnish with parsley and serve hot.
Note if fresh pumpkin is not available, use puree` from the can (1 lb.).

SERVING SIZE: one cup
TOTAL SERVINGS: fourteen

AMOUNT PER SERVING:

Calories	138.58 kcal
Total fat	7.01 g
Cholesterol	1.71 mg
Sodium	563.51 mg
Total carbohydrate	19.50 g
Dietary fiber	55.52 g
Protein	2.17 g

NOTE:
Pumpkins are grown all around the world for a variety of reasons ranging from
Agricultural purposes (such as animal feed) to commercial and ornamental sales. Out of the seven continents, only Antarctica is unable to produce pumpkins; the biggest international producers of pumpkins include the United States, Mexico, India, and China. The traditional American pumpkin is the Connecticut Field variety.

SPLIT PEA SOUP (bazella m'kassara)

INGREDIENTS:
2 cups split peas, 2 quarts water
1 cup sliced celery, 1 cup diced onion
1 cup chopped carrots, 1 cup diced potatoes
5 cloves minced garlic
2 bay leaves
1 cup chopped parsley
1 tsp. crushed oregano
1 tsp. crushed basil
1 tsp. Italian seasoning
1 tsp. salt, 1 pinch cayenne pepper powder

COOKING:
In a 4 quart cooking pot, combine all the ingredients.
Bring to a boil, and then reduce the heat to low.
Cover and cook for forty minutes or until the split peas are cooked through.
Remove the bay leaves before serving.

SERVING SIZE: one cup
TOTAL SERVING: Thirteen

AMOUNT PER SERVING:

Calories	115.96 kcal
Total fat	0.45 g
Cholesterol	0.00 mg
Sodium	218.93 mg
Total carbohydrate	27.90 g
Dietary Fiber	11.08 g
Protein	8.69 g

NOTE:
Serve hot with a squeeze of lemon and toasted pita bread.

TAHINEH SAUCE (tarator)

INGREDIENTS:
½ cup sesame seeds paste (tahineh)
3 garlic cloves
¼ cup fresh lemon juice
¼ cup water
½ tsp. salt
¼ cup chopped fine parsley (optional)

COOKING:
Combine tahineh paste and lemon juice and mix well.
Add a little water if the sauce is not soft enough.
Add the garlic and the salt and mix well.
Then add the parsley if you desire.

SERVING SIZE: 1/8 cup
TOTAL SERVINGS: nine

_____

AMOUNT PER SERVING:
Calories	0.80 kcal
Total fat	7.45 g
Cholesterol	0.00 mg
Sodium	134.80 mg
Total carbohydrate	4.58 g
Dietary fiber	1.37 g
Protein	2.60 g

NOTE:
Tahini is an Arabic word loaned to the English language. Tahineh is more accurate; tahineh is derived from the word tahin which means grind. The standard Arabic word is tahineh in most Arabic dialects. In Syria and Lebanon, the word sounds like (t'heeneh). Tahineh is used in many Middle Eastern dishes like hummos, baba ghannouj, m'tabbal, sauce and others. Tahineh contain Vitamin A, thiamin, folate, calcium, iron, magnesium, phosphorus, potassium, zinc, copper and manganese.

TOMATO SOUP (Shorabet banadora)

INGREDIENTS:

1 can chicken broth (14 oz.)
1 can tomato sauce (15 oz.)
1/8 cup I Can't Believe It's Not Butter!®
1 medium size chopped onion
½ cup chopped parsley
1 tsp. salt
¼ tsp. cinnamon
¼ tsp. allspice
1 tsp. oregano (optional)
1½ cups water

COOKING:

Sauté the onion with the butter then add tomato sauce, chicken broth, water, and bring to a boil.
Reduce the heat and add salt, allspice, oregano, cinnamon, and cook for 15 minutes.
Mix in the parsley and serve hot.

SERVING SIZE: one cup
TOTAL SERVINGS: five

AMOUNT PER SERVING:

Calories	126.55 kcal
Total fat	8.50 g
Cholesterol	0.00 mg
Sodium	1169.70 mg
Total carbohydrate	10.64 g
Dietary fiber	2.18 g
Protein	3.32 g

NOTE:

Enjoy with toasted pita bread chips.

VEGETABLE SOUP (Shorabet khudra)

INGREDIENTS:

1/2 cup I Can't Believe It's Not Butter! ®
1 can tomato sauce (15 oz.), 1 large chopped onion
1 large chopped potato, 1 cup cauliflower florets
1 cup chopped green beans, 1 cup petite peas
1 cup chopped carrots, 1 cup elbow macaroni
1 tsp. salt, 1 tsp. allspice, 12 cups water

COOKING:

Sauté the onion with butter in a large pot and add salt and allspice.
Add the water and bring to a boil; then reduce the heat and cook for five to ten minutes.
Add the rest of the ingredients and bring to a boil again; then reduce the heat and cook for another forty-five minutes or until the vegetables are tender. Serve hot with a squeeze of fresh lemon.

SERVING SIZE: one cup
TOTAL SERVINGS: eleven

AMOUNT PER SERVING:

Calories	112.00 kcal
Total fat	3.80 g
Cholesterol	0.00 mg
Sodium	182.85 mg
Total carbohydrate	17.55 g
Dietary fiber	3.02 g
Protein	2.83 g

NOTE:

Vegetables are eaten in a variety of ways: as part of the main meal or as a snack.
The nutritional content of vegetables varies considerably, though generally they contain little fat and a varying proportion of vitamins.
Vegetables also contain a great variety of other phytochemicals, some of which have been claimed to have antioxidant, antibacterial and antifungal benefits. Eating vegetables helps lower the risk of heart diseases and Type II diabetes.

HELPFUL INFORMATION

MAKING RENDERED BUTTER
Place four pounds of sweet butter in a soup pot and melt it.
Bring the butter to a boil and skim the froth that appears on the top of the butter.
Reduce the heat to low and sprinkle the top of the butter with a half cup of bulgur.
Shut off the heat, stir the bulgur and set aside for the bulgur to settle to the bottom of the pot.
Drain the clear butter and store in a glass jar and refrigerate; discard the bulgur.

MAKING ZAATAR
¼ cup dried and crushed thyme; 2 tbsp. dried and crushed oregano. One tbsp. dried and crushed basil; 2 tbsp. dried and crushed marjoram. Two tbsp. sumac, 1 tsp. salt, ¼ cup roasted sesame seeds. Place all the ingredients, except the sesame seeds, in a clean coffee grinder and grind them. Place the mixture in a container and mix in the sesame seeds and refrigerate.

MIXING ALLSPICE
4 tsp. ground black pepper, 1 tsp. cardamom, 3 tsp. ground cloves, 3 tsp. ground coriander,
3 tsp. cumin, 3 tsp. ground nutmeg, 2 tsp. paprika, 3 tsp. cinnamon.
Mix all the ingredients together and store them in a clean glass jar.

FREEZING LIQUID
You can freeze milk, orange juice, apple juice and many liquids in plastic containers.
Make sure that you leave 20 per cent of the volume empty because liquid expands at the freezing Temperature.

FREEZING GRAPE LEAVES
Wash the fresh grape leaves very well then spread them out to dry. Gather all the grape leaves after they dry, pile one leaf over the other. Roll the pile like a cylinder and wrap it with plastic wrap.
Wrap the package again with aluminum foil and freeze it. (A count of seventy leaves in a
package usually used with one meatless stuffing recipe. Spare ten grape leaves to be used to cover the bottom of the pot and the top of the rolled grape leaves. (See stuffed grape leaves recipe in the meatless chapter.)

CPSIA information can be obtained
at www.ICGtesting.com
Printed in the USA
BVHW011539290620
582597BV00007B/137

9 780985 001018